A YOUNG HISTORIAN BOOK

Modern China

The Chinese long thought of their country as the "Middle Kingdom" - the centre of the world. They still do today, despite many changes since 1842 when our story begins.

Early traders – lured by silk, tea, porcelain, spices and medicines – brought with them new ideas which many Chinese seized upon because they longed to be rid of the foreign Manchu emperors. Soon, revolutionary dreams of freedom, modernization and even democracy swept through the country.

But as Cornelia Spencer shows, if the Nationalist revolution of Sun Yat-sen in 1911 failed, it only increased the demand for change; and the Russian revolution of 1917 added to the ferment of ideas among young Chinese. After the First World War, Chinese disappointment at the peace terms gave birth to the May the Fourth Movement. It fired the country. A renaissance of new ideas, new styles of writing, almost a new language, sprang from the hunger for modernization.

In the 1930s, however, Nationalists and Communists fought a bitter civil war for control of the new China, and it took a Japanese invasion to force them together even temporarily. After 1945 a herculean effort was made to unify China permanently, but, as the author shows, it failed entirely. After a bloody struggle Chiang Kai-shek's Nationalists were pushed from the mainland to the island of Taiwan (Formosa), while the Communists under Chairman Mao Tse-tung hold real power in Peking today.

By the same author
ANCIENT CHINA

Other books for the Young Historian, uniform with this volume
ANCIENT CHINA   *Cornelia Spencer*
ANCIENT CRETE   *Frances Wilkins*
ANCIENT EGYPT   *Roger Lancelyn Green*
ANCIENT JAPAN   *J. E. Kidder*
ANCIENT RUSSIA   *Melvin C. Wren*
ANCIENT SCANDINAVIA   *George L. Proctor*
ANCIENT GREECE   *Roger Lancelyn Green*
IMPERIAL ROME   *H. E. L. Mellersh*
REPUBLICAN ROME   *E. Royston Pike*
THE ANCIENT MAYA   *C. A. Burland*
THE REFORMATION   *L. W. Cowie*
THE RENAISSANCE   *George Bull*
MODERN JAPAN   *Brian Powell*

THE YOUNG HISTORIAN BOOKS
Edited by Patrick Rooke MA BSC (ECON)

Modern China

BY CORNELIA SPENCER

DRAWINGS BY ELIZABETH HAMMOND

RUPERT HART-DAVIS EDUCATIONAL PUBLICATIONS
3 Upper James Street Golden Square London W1

Acknowledgments

The author and publishers wish to express their thanks to the following for permission to reproduce copyright material on the pages mentioned: King Features Syndicate, New York, page 83; Library of Congress, pages 10, 20, 84 (top), 89, 97, 101, 103 and 104; The Mansell Collection, pages 8, 14, 16, 18, 24, 25, 36, 41 (two), 86 and 87; United Press International, New York, 74 and 75; US Army Photographs, pages 80 and 84 (bottom). The map on page 30 was drawn by Elizabeth Hammond, and the map on pages 56–57 supplied by The John Day Company, New York. The author supplied the photographs on pages 15, 17, 21 and 49.

COPYRIGHT © 1969 BY CORNELIA SPENCER

SBN 298 76486 5

Phototypeset by BAS Printers Limited, Wallop, Hampshire
Printed in Great Britain by Unwin Brothers Ltd, London and Woking

Contents

    List of Illustrations   6
    Introduction   9

PART ONE – Keeping Out the Rest of the World 1842–95

1. Why the Western World Wanted to Trade with China   13
2. China Wants to Look Modern Without Becoming So   20
3. The Influence of Japan   23
4. The United States Tries to Keep China Whole   27

PART TWO – Reform and Revolution 1895–1943

5. A First Effort to Save Herself by Reforms Fails   31
6. A Second Effort to Save Herself by Reforms Is Too Late   34
7. A Revolution That Failed   38
8. China and the First World War   43
9. The Nationalist Revolution   46
10. General Chiang Kai-shek and the New Capital   52
11. Incident at Sian   62
12. The Great Migration: Free China   66
13. The United States Comes to the Aid of China: The War of the South Pacific, 1941–5   72

PART THREE – Two Chinas 1943–66

14. Nationalists Face Communists   81
15. Mainland China   93
16. At the Crossroads   99
    Table of Main Dates   108
    Suggestions for Further Reading   110
    Index   111

List of Illustrations

The Great Wall of China	8
Marco Polo	10
Feeding silk worms	11
A mandarin on a visit	12
East India House, London	14
Chinese pirate ship	15
Signing the Treaty of Nanking, 1842	16
Foreign business houses in Canton	17
Four Chinese figures	18
The Western Gate in Peking	19
European conducting a Chinese artillery class	20
Buddhist gargoyle and Christian church	21
The first Chinese railway train, 1876	24
Viceroy Li Hung-chang	25
Map: The opening up of China by the West	**30**
Opium smokers	36
A Hong Kong side street	39
Yuan Shih-k'ai	41
Dr Sun Yat-sen	41
The tomb of Sun Yat-sen	49
Map of China: between the wars	**56–57**
Chungking residents await air raid warning	74
Madame Chiang Kai-shek in Chungking	75
Admiral Mountbatten and General Stilwell, 1944	80
Refugee train leaving eastern China, 1944	83
Refugee Chinese children, 1945	84
The first convoy over the Ledo-Burma road, 1945	84
General Chiang Kai-shek	86
General George C. Marshall	87
UNRRA flour being unloaded at Shanghai	89
Prime Minister Chou En-lai	97
A modern iron works near Peking	101
Scene from *The Wild Goose*, a Chinese classic opera	103
Tsien San-tsiang, the Chinese nuclear physicist	104
Chairman Mao Tse-tung	106

PART ONE

Keeping Out the Rest of the World
1842–95

Introduction

The Chinese have always called their country "The Middle Kingdom", because they believed it to be the centre of the world, perhaps even of the universe. Had not their culture been superior for hundreds of years to that of countries around them? Outsiders travelled across deserts and mountains along China's northern and western inland frontiers, and traders and missionaries braved great oceans and choppy seas on her east and south just to get a chance to study, copy, or bargain for it.

The Middle Kingdom

The long, unbroken thread of China's history and culture began almost 2,000 years before the time of Jesus. Although Mongols and Manchus have sat on the throne in Peking, China has never actually been any other country's colony or been occupied by another nation.

The Chinese people used the ideas that came to them from other parts of the world to enrich their own life. When Buddhism arrived from India between the third and sixth centuries AD, the Chinese studied it and adapted it to suit themselves. It touched their architecture, dotting the countryside with pagodas and Buddhist temples, but it did not change the direction of their cultural development. Instead, it was swallowed up by it. Other cultures that came into China were used in the same way, becoming Chinese.

Nearby neighbours were the first people who tried to push their way into China. These were nomad tribes and rough barbarians from the north and northwest. Chinese emperors began to build the Great Wall to keep them out. The Japanese were always eager to learn of their great neighbour. The first arrivals from the Western world were Portuguese and Spanish traders, who were followed by French, British, and American businessmen and then by missionaries. They were large, swarthy, red-faced, or high-nosed. The Chinese thought them unimportant and repulsive.

Visitors

(*opposite*) The Great Wall of China, crowning mountains and dwarfing human beings

A drawing from an old map, depicting Marco Polo on his way to Peking

China's secrets

What was it that these people from the outside wanted to get from China? They wanted her secret of raising silk and weaving it, her methods of printing and papermaking, of producing porcelains and pottery, her architectural designs, her painting and poetry, and her comforting philosophy. Some of the Westerners were sure that they could make China much richer if she would trade with their countries. Some declared that they could save her people's souls from their sins through religion. But China did not feel the need of either of these things. She did not crave the articles the outside world offered her in trade, because she believed that her own were superior. She was not interested in a religion based on repenting, because she did not think of her people as sinners. The Middle Kingdom did not want anything from any country unless it came as tribute from a subject state. Let other nations bring tribute to her court in Peking if they chose to do so.

Although China told herself she would never change, new ideas came in with traders and especially with missionaries. As time passed, some Chinese leaders, particularly young men who had gone abroad to study, began to demand modernization. They declared that even though the Manchus, who had taken the Chinese throne in 1644 and still held it, were careful to preserve Chinese culture, they were actually foreign rulers. Revolutionary thinkers appealed to Chinese hatred of outside domination. They called for rebellion against it.

New ideas

This book is about how China changed from an ancient empire into a new kind of nation. That change took a form that was more dramatic and thorough than even the

Feeding silk worms. The silk worms are being carried on the tray

The rich and powerful mandarins travelled by litter and surrounded by attendants

revolutionaries expected. It affected the lives of one-fourth of the modern world's people. As Communists, the Chinese have more than ever shut themselves away from the outside world. China is to them more than ever the centre of the world, a modernized Middle Kingdom.

CHAPTER ONE

Why the Western World Wanted to Trade with China

The story of modern China does not go by dynasties, like that of ancient China. It is no longer a chronicle of ruling families, but an argument between old and respected ways of thinking and the new ideas that got into China, in spite of all that was done to keep them out.

These new ideas first appeared along with British traders of the East India Company who were experienced in the Far East. Although Portuguese and Dutch traders had preceded them there, the British trade had been chartered by Queen Elizabeth I in 1600. In later centuries a great volume of commerce had developed between East and West, and a strong British colonial empire had gradually been set up in India. By the middle of the nineteenth century China could no longer resist the determination of Britain and other Western countries to establish trade. This determination increased rapidly because a great pressure was building up. It was caused mainly by the industrial revolution, which first developed in Britain and produced large quantities of goods for the markets of the world. Britain had to exchange the output of her factories for raw materials, but China did not want what those factories made. Britain could buy India's raw materials, manufacture India's cotton into cloth in British mills, and sell it back to her, but China wove her own fine silks and satins, grew and prepared her own tea ready for the teapot, and left nothing for the factories of the industrial revolution to do. At last Britain solved the dilemma by setting up a three-way trade. Her East India Company accepted Indian opium as payment for some of Britain's manufactured goods and then shipped the opium to China to pay for China's tea and silk. The young United States sent her clipper ships to China for tea and silk and porcelains, paying for them in furs and whale oil. But she had the same trouble as Britain in finding enough to give China in ex-

Britain

East India House in London, the old headquarters of the East India Company

change for what she wanted to buy. She also began to use opium as money, picking it up in the Middle East or wherever she could get hold of it, although the United States' industrial development was not yet pressing for an outlet for its manufactured goods.

The Treaty of Nanking

The First Foreign War with Britain, or the First Opium War, broke out over opium in 1839, when Peking decided to stop the trade. The war ended with the Treaty of Nanking in 1842. Although the British troops – including the East Indians they employed – never numbered more than 15,000, they were highly successful along the sea coast and the Yangtze River because the Chinese government could not inspire its people to resist. Most Chinese did not realize how change was pushing on China's doors. The emperor was so afraid his people would revolt against his dynasty, which was Manchu and thus foreign, that he could hardly hope to marshal them against any other barbarians (as all foreigners were called). The Chinese had not yet begun to look out at the world. When they did, they would begin to feel a pull towards unity, or nationalism. Now the treaty of Nanking meant only humiliation and hatred of foreigners, especially the British. Humiliation even overshadowed the real significance of the crumbling resistance to outside trade.

The Western world had won a beachhead in China, as it had long wanted to do. The treaty gave Britain a lease on Hong Kong and special rights in five important ports, Canton, Amoy, Foochow, Ningpo, and Shanghai. In these places, foreigners, or Westerners, could live under the legal care of their own resident officials, or consuls, instead of being subject to Chinese courts. This privilege was the beginning of what is known as extraterritoriality. A year after the treaty was drawn up, Britain was able to get special tariff rates that assured her the same benefits as any other nation who made agreements with China. This was called the most-favoured-nation treatment. The United States soon sent a man named Caleb Cushing to China as her commissioner to ask for the same privileges granted to Britain, and before long, France did the same. Belgium and Sweden also demanded these rights.

The Treaty Ports

European traders were long regarded with hostility by the Chinese, and attacked by Chinese pirates. This Chinese pirate ship was sketched by a Chinese at Canton (1856)

The doors of China were forced open by the signing of the historic Treaty of Nanking in 1842

Traders and missionaries, protected by the treaties, began to pour into China. They brought in strange products and new religious and political ideas. New ways of thinking first took hold in China's secret societies. They were the places where rebellions were often started.

The Taiping Rebellion

After the First Opium War, secret societies in the southern province Kwangtung were especially full of resentment against the new treaty. The war had so weakened the power of the throne in Peking that it was less than ever able to control the country's great expanse or curb the political strength of secret societies. A mentally unbalanced man used some parts of the teachings of the Christian missionaries and decided that God was calling him to lead a rebellion. He named the movement the Great Peace, or Taiping, Rebellion. Poor, oppressed, and uneducated people, some of whom belonged to non-Chinese tribes in South China became his followers. They swept northward and reached the Yangtze River Valley, where they ruined city after city. In 1853 they captured Nanking and held it for ten years. They were at last defeated by an able Chinese leader named Tseng Kuo-fan, with the help of an English major, Charles George Gordon, who became known as Chinese Gordon, and a peculiar American named Frederick Townsend Ward. When the rebellion was finally over, it had cost 1,000,000 lives and devastated several provinces.

The Taiping Rebellion increased the power of Western countries in China. Collection of maritime duties, or customs on imported goods, was now put in the hands of British officials so that it could be better controlled. In 1863 Sir Robert Hart became the able head of this system, which was soon producing reliable income for the court in Peking. The agency also charted China's seacoast and built lighthouses to aid navigation. Later it started a modern postal system. Part of the income from duties was used to set up and finance a new office called the Tsungli Yamen. Its business was to handle all foreign affairs. While all of these developments strengthened the imperial government, they still involved foreigners in China's high offices. A growing spirit of rebellion was fostered by such methods of progress, even though some conditions had been improved.

War between China and Britain broke out again in 1857 over a small incident, and British and French forces seized Canton. The next year Britain, the United States, France, and Russia each sent a squadron of ships north to threaten Peking from its port city, Tientsin. China submitted to their pressure and accepted the Treaty of Tientsin in 1858. Russian and American representatives demanded that they get the same rights as France and Britain, even though they were not involved in this war, which was known as the Second Foreign War, or the Second Opium War. The main provisions of the new treaty legalized trade in opium and promised that diplomatic representatives of foreign countries could live in Peking, that foreigners could travel wherever they liked in China, that missionaries and Chinese Christians could practice their religion, and that foreign merchant ships

The Treaty of Tientsin

Foreign business houses, or "hongs" in Canton, flying the flags of their nations, as seen from offshore

could go up and down the Yangtze River. It also opened more ports to foreign shipping.

When representatives of Britain and France arrived to assume their posts in Peking, as the treaty permitted, they found that their passage from Tientsin to the capital was blocked. War began all over again. Peking was occupied by foreign troops, and the beautiful Summer Palace was burned. China had, in the end, to sign embarrassing papers that promised that she would carry out the provisions of the Treaty of Tientsin and go even farther. From now on, foreigners were to be allowed to hold land under long leases and to establish religious centres, as well as to trade as they liked, free from Chinese interference.

Outcome As a result of the Taiping Rebellion and this second foreign war, foreign power became stronger than ever in China. Foreign officials collected her customs, held land, set up business houses. They sent their ships up and down the Yangtze and had representatives in Peking and in port cities

Lifelike Chinese figures: from left to right, bronze man, wooden beggar, ivory Goddess of Mercy on a cloud, wooden farmer and toad

The Western Gate in the walls of Peking, a busy thoroughfare

along the river and coast, who were subject to no authority but that of their own national courts. Every foreigner in China was still a citizen of his own country. No matter how badly he behaved or what crime he committed, he could not be tried in a Chinese court.

The Ch'ing dynasty, which had been established by the Manchus in 1644, was threatened, but a strong leader prolonged its life. This leader was the Empress Dowager Tz'u Hsi, regent for her son, the emperor, until he came of age. She had played an important role in the Taiping Rebellion by dispatching Tseng Kuo-fan to rescue Nanking. When her son died, soon after he had ascended to the throne in 1895, she managed to keep the power in her hands by having a child made heir to the throne so that she would be regent once more. This child was to become Emperor Kuang Hsu.

Tz'u Hsi

CHAPTER TWO

China Wants to Look Modern Without Becoming So

The empress dowager realized that China had to find ways of meeting the pressure of foreign governments. Both Tseng Kuo-fan and another official named Li Hung-chang could be depended upon for help because they each wanted to start reforms. They were urging the building of arsenals where Western ships and munitions could be produced and the translating of Western books on science and technology into the Chinese language for schools. They supported the foreign office, Tsungli Yamen, and began a programme of training Chinese personnel especially for official positions.

In 1866 Peking sent its first official observer abroad. The following year, Anson Burlingame, the American foreign minister in Peking, headed China's first formal embassy ever to visit Western capitals. By 1880 China had representatives

A European instructor conducting an artillery class at Tientsin Imperial University, part of China's attempts to modernize

A Buddhist gargoyle and Christian mission church steeple overlook the roofs of an inland Chinese city

in most large capitals, and by 1890 the empress dowager was willing to receive foreign envoys at her court, although she firmly maintained the viewpoint that they were bringing tribute from their inferior countries.

The number of Christian missionaries in China had grown rapidly under the protection of the trade treaties. Schools and hospitals could be built on land that was now available under long leases and protected by the rights of extraterritoriality. By 1890 there were several thousand missionaries in China. They had led about 500,000 Chinese to become Roman Catholics, and another 50,000 were members of Protestant churches. Mission schools were crowded, because modern subjects had become popular. Students begged Westerners to teach them the English language, for it had become the key to going abroad or getting ahead in almost any business or profession.

Christian missions

In Canton a Christian Chinese doctor named Sun Yat-sen dreamed of getting rid of the foreign Ch'ing dynasty and establishing a republic. He heard about the reforms that were being made in Peking. Li Hung-chang, who had become viceroy, was known as a progressive man. Sun Yat-sen and one of his friends carefully prepared a long petition to Li Hung-chang, urging him to go farther than reforms and consider a new form of government. They took the petition to Peking themselves but were unable to get an

Sun Yat-sen

appointment with the viceroy, though they waited many days and tried again and again. When they left the city at last, bitterly disappointed, with their document still undelivered, it seemed to them that China's only hope lay in revolution, rather than reform.

Manchu aims   The Manchu leaders succeeded in making some significant changes. But they were really intended only to strengthen their own system, because they still firmly believed that what they had was better than anything the West could offer. These leaders hoped to be able to take such innovations as arms and machines from the West but reject other things, such as industrialization and new ideas about institutions and government. If some of them knew that halfway measures like these were really useless, they did not dare say so. They would not have been listened to, anyway, because only a few leaders were willing to go even as far as the reformers were going.

CHAPTER THREE

The Influence of Japan

Japan was reacting very differently to change. Although all foreigners except for a small group of Dutchmen had been banned for more than 200 years during the Tokugawa period (1603–1867), and no Japanese had been allowed to go abroad, Japan had begun full-scale modernization in 1868. She invited American and European advisers to come, began to build railroads, and even adopted Western styles in official dress. Japanese students came and went from the West and brought home a steady stream of new ideas. The government started to experiment with first steps in representative organizations and in setting up political parties.

Japan modernizes

By 1895 China was next door to a nation that had done what she herself was still hesitating to do. Japan had accepted what the West had to offer and was moving forward quickly into a place among the great powers. China still hung back, hoping to preserve her past and make only surface reforms. She was suddenly shaken from this plan when Japan went to war with her over Korea.

An insurrection erupted in Korea, and Chinese forces were sent in to put it down. Li Hung-chang, the viceroy and reformer, said that Peking ought to take this chance to demonstrate that Korea was actually part of China. Japan responded to this by moving swiftly into Korea, defeating the Chinese forces there, and then pushing on to invade Shantung Province, Manchuria, and ports controlling the sea approaches to Peking. The war was soon over, and Japan was in a position to demand a settlement by treaty. What came was the Treaty of Shimonoseki. This gave Korea so-called independence, while it demanded that China forfeit her rights to Formosa, the Pescadores islands nearby, and the Liaotung Peninsula in Manchuria. China was also required to pay a large indemnity. Korea's independence was actually a threat, because she was not strong enough to

Korea

Chinese weakness

defend herself against Japan's probable aggression.

The outcome of the first Chino-Japanese War was disastrous for China in itself, but the fact that it had revealed how weak she really was, was even worse. She was antiquated, compared with the bristling, modern, militarized Japan. The outside powers, seeing this, now started to carve China up so that each could get what it wanted and buffer itself against others who were doing the same thing.

Russian, British, French, and German bankers began to scramble madly for shares in the loans China had to get to pay her indemnity and war costs. China believed that this behaviour showed the true barbarity of Western nations. While some of the Westerners had been teaching brotherhood, others of the same countries were out to take all they could get. Missionaries could not separate themselves from the actions of other citizens of their countries. They were part of the system of extraterritoriality, which supplied them with military and legal protection.

China's need for loans to cover indemnities involved even more than this. In the 1895 scramble, Russia secured rights

Starting the first railway train in China at Shanghai, opening the Woosung line in 1876

Viceroy Li Hung-chang

to bring her Trans-Siberian Railroad down through Manchuria, instead of staying in her own territory by following the Amur and Ussuri Rivers. She also made claims in Korea. France, too, extended her rights in Indochina, now Vietnam, Laos, and Cambodia; these resulted from the settlement made in the Treaty of Tientsin in 1862 and from mining privileges she already held in China. Britain was alarmed when she observed what was going to these countries and demanded concessions along the border, between China and Burma. India, next door to Burma, was already under British control. In 1897 Germany seized the city of Tsingtao, an important seaport on the coast of Shantung Province. In a few months she demanded the harbour itself, as well as enough land around it to control it completely for the duration of a ninety-nine-year lease. Before long, she had managed to get mining and railroad rights throughout the province.

The 1895 scramble

Russia decided to take Port Arthur and Dairen, cities on the Liaotung Peninsula. Not much time passed before she had a twenty-five-year lease on these two ports and areas surrounding them. Britain, meanwhile, took over a smaller Shantung port called Weihaiwei and in the south, got a ninety-nine-year lease on more of Kowloon, the promontory opposite the island of Hong Kong. France extended her holdings over Kwangchow Bay near Hainan Island. A port on this island had already been opened to foreign trade by the Treaty of Tientsin, and in 1897 France succeeded in getting China's promise never to let a third party move into Hainan. Now France herself was spreading out. The pattern of each nation laying claim to whatever it could get from the weak empire continued like a nightmare. China seemed to be paralyzed, unable to hold off her attackers.

Spheres of influence

The foreign nations began to build invisible fences around areas, or spheres of influence, that each wanted to develop for herself. Britain claimed the provinces along the Yangtze River as her sphere; France added the province bordering on what she already held in the South as her sphere; Japan got a promise that no other power would be allowed to enter the province of Fukien on the mainland, opposite Formosa; Russia claimed all the area north of the Great Wall as under her control.

The division of China among the great powers went beyond the leasing of special ports and lands adjacent to them and defining spheres of influence. The nations began to compete with one another in providing the money to build railroads, which meant that each would control its own line and much of the trade in the area that it crossed.

In spite of all that was going on, the Chinese people, as a whole, still went on living as they always had, sure that their culture was the best, their country the world's greatest.

CHAPTER FOUR

The United States Tries to Keep China Whole

The scramble among foreign countries for privileges in China threatened to tear the empire apart. Even those who were benefiting from what was going on began to realize this.

Although the United States had been so involved in her own affairs at home that she had not played any important role in setting up spheres of influence in China, she now studied the treaties that China had made with other countries. According to what was called the most-favoured-nation plan, all foreign countries had to share alike in whatever they could get from China in the form of rights and concessions. The United States had more than once benefited from agreements to which she had not been a party, but a kind of junior partner to Britain. In 1899 the American Secretary of State, John Hay, proposed an Open Door Policy to stop the competition among foreign powers in China. This had two purposes. The first was to check further division of China into spheres of influence. The second was to give all powers an equal chance in developing China. John Hay proposed, too, that China be allowed to collect her own customs in the spheres of influence.

Open Door Policy

When the United States made these proposals through John Hay, some people praised her for trying to protect China, but the proposal was really intended only to set up some rules for carrying on foreign trade and development in China. The United States was continuing the same policy she had followed toward China for a long time. Her trade had begun in Canton, along with that of England's East India Company. In 1844 the United States had made her first treaty with China, growing out of the British Treaty of Nanking, after the First Opium War, and benefiting from it.

The great difference between the United States' China trade and that of Britain was that for a long time it did not involve the United States Government at all. It was carried on by a few adventurous men who were intrigued by the Far East and its products, rather than by big companies. The home government did not pay much attention to what a handful of pioneers were doing in the Orient unless some special situation demanded its attention. The Open Door Policy was not proposed against the background of any steady policy that the United States had maintained down through the years, but against a background of different ones that had been used to fit special situations.

American colonies

In 1898, at the very time the Open Door Policy was being suggested, the United States took on Hawaii and, a month after that, colonies resulting from a treaty made with Spain at the end of the Spanish-American War. These were Puerto Rico, Guam, and the Philippines. Soon, another treaty gave her part of Samoa. America had, in this short time, acquired colonial lands larger in area than those the powers were competing for in China, although she had not made deliberate plans to colonize. She had acquired these territories in much the same way that she had secured the advantages of treaties fought for by other countries in China – without exactly planning or intending to do so. However, the United States did not seem to think of applying the Open Door Policy which she had proposed for China to the question of the colonies which she herself was annexing.

The proposed policy did not end the scramble among the powers in China. John Hay's plan as yet lacked strength; it was not made legally binding on any power for another twenty years.

PART TWO

Reform and Revolution
1895–1943

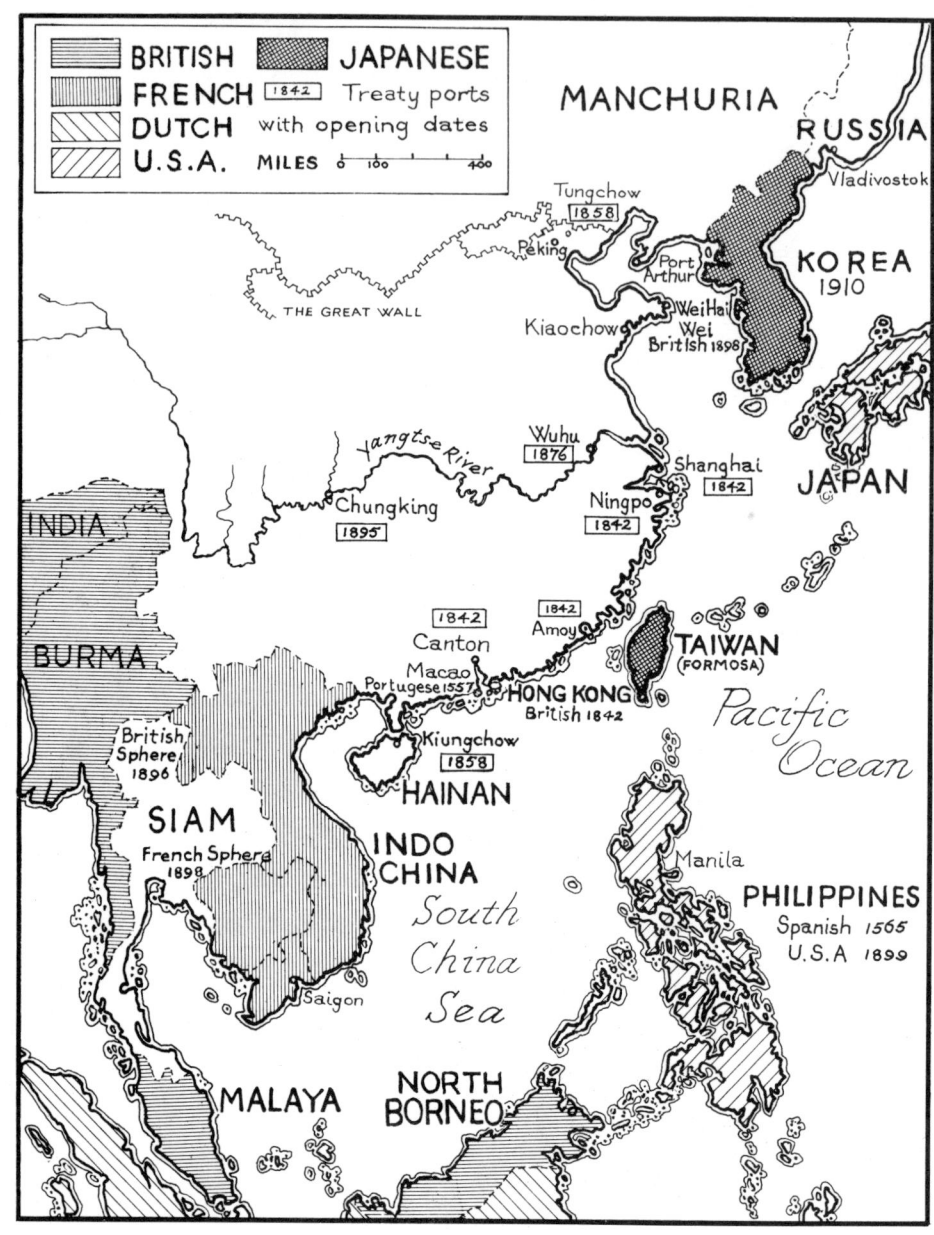

The opening up of China by the West. The Treaty Ports were open to Europeans from the dates given

CHAPTER FIVE

A First Effort to Save Herself by Reforms Fails

The First Chino-Japanese War in 1895 convinced China that she would have to take more drastic steps if she wanted to maintain her position as the Middle Kingdom. The Empress Dowager Tz'u Hsi's policies of sending students abroad to study and an embassy to the Western world under Anson Burlingame leading to placing Chinese envoys in foreign capitals, were still not enough. The two government schools which had been set up to train diplomats did not satisfy the cry, "Reform!" which was quickly becoming a slogan. Clubs to promote political reform were springing up, claiming that such reform had been the key to Japan's success. A pamphlet called "Learn" declared that China could modernize her life and her government, without sacrificing her ancient culture, if she really wanted to do so.

The Hundred Days of Reform

Two men stepped forward to lead a dramatic reform movement. One of these was K'ang Yu-wei, a brilliant scholar; the other, Liang Ch'i-chao, one of his students, called a master of written Chinese. They presented themselves to young Emperor Kuang Hsu, even though they knew that he was always under the watchful eye of the dowager. He read their proposals and talked with them a long time, because he was convinced that something had to be done at once to keep China whole and to maintain her superiority. The emperor enthusiastically made great plans for new policies, with the help of the reformers, and announced them to the country. June, July, and August of 1898 came to be known as the Hundred Days of Reform.

While the plans proposed seem moderate in our day, they were sweeping reforms for China at that time in her history. They were to modernize the civil service examinations and to establish a nationwide system of schools, which would teach Western, as well as Chinese, subjects, headed by an imperial university. China had never before had a public school system. Special military schools were to give instruction in modern military tactics, leading to the organization of a national army. Law courts were to be reorganized; new government bureaus in commerce, agriculture, and the arts were to be established.

The ambitious reforms were never even begun, because the empress dowager discovered what Emperor Kuang Hsu was planning and quickly took the controls of government from him. He was so restricted that he was practically a prisoner. Many of the reformers were executed, and their announced plans annulled. The empress dowager went even farther, because the threat of real change terrified her and seemed to blind her to reason. She now decided to get rid of all foreigners, once and for all. They were the source of China's troubles. She promoted an underground plan of attack, and when the word went around, secret societies and groups of rowdies joined it. One of the secret societies had the name Righteous Harmony Fists, or Boxers.

The Boxer Uprising

The Boxers, supported by the empress dowager, began to persecute foreigners and Chinese Christians, who were thought of as followers of the foreigners, in the autumn of 1899. Western governments sent extra troops to Peking to protect their nationals, under the extraterritorial arrangement early in the next year. When they took over the Taku forts on the coast to keep the sea to Peking open, the empress dowager suddenly ordered all foreigners executed. The German foreign minister to China was murdered, and other foreign diplomatic representatives and their staffs were detained under fire in the legation section of Peking. Hundreds of missionaries and thousands of Chinese Christians scattered through the northeastern part of the country were killed. The foreign powers tried to explain that the purpose of their troop movements was not to wage war on China, but only to protect their nationals. Many Chinese officials, understanding the situation, tried to counsel the empress dowager, but she did not seem to hear them.

In August, 1900, an international military force took Peking, and the imperial court fled to the city of Sian. The situation of the besieged foreigners in the capital was desperate. When the infuriated foreign troops entered Peking, they went wild and looted its beautiful palaces before they freed the many frightened foreigners.

War had not been declared, but the outside powers felt that they had a right to demand payment from China for what had happened. Some of the terms were: officials who were responsible were to be punished; memorial monuments to the foreigners who had been murdered were to be built at the locations where the murders had occurred; a formal mission was to go to Berlin to apologize for the death of the German foreign minister; civil service examinations were to be suspended for five years in towns where foreigners had been either mistreated or killed; no arms were to be imported to China for two years; an indemnity, or fine, of $330,000,000, spread over a period of thirty-nine years, was to be paid to the nations involved. The cost of the Boxer Rebellion was crushing.

All attempts to save China and keep her whole had failed. The Open Door Policy had helped in some ways, but a time had come when nothing from the outside could save her. She had to adjust to a changing world and take her place in it or else be a prey to it. After the Boxer Rebellion, China was in a worse position with the Western nations than ever before.

Retribution

CHAPTER SIX

A Second Effort to Save Herself by Reforms Is Too Late

Russia Russia was now China's most urgent problem. Manchuria was in a state of disorder, and Russia sent in troops, who soon occupied a large part of southern Manchuria. Britain was alarmed, always fearing that Russian power would become too strong in the Far East. Japan also was nervous about Russia, because she threatened Korea, which Japan now considered her own. In 1902 the British and Japanese Governments drew up an alliance that joined their forces against Russia, while the United States, too, added her protest against Russia. Threatened by these three great powers, Russia agreed to respect the trade rights of all other nations in Manchuria and gradually to withdraw her troops from there. But she delayed moving her troops for such a long time that Japan tried, without success, to negotiate directly with the Russian Government about it.

In February, 1904, Japan went to war with Russia. China watched, amazed when her small neighbour captured Port Arthur, drove the Russians out of Manchuria, and then destroyed the Russian fleet. The United States was watching, too, and in 1905 President Theodore Roosevelt stepped in as a mediator. The war ended with the Treaty of Portsmouth. Russia was required to recognize Japan's authority in Korea and to give up her railroad rights in the Liaotung Peninsula, as well as to cede to Japan half of a large offshore island, Sakhalin.

As far as China was concerned, Japan had simply taken Russia's place in Manchuria. Japan had certainly not shown any concern about China's rights. China now complained, and Japan answered by declaring that she had fought harder for and spent more to develop Manchuria than had China. What did a frightening statement like this mean for the future? Chinese leaders asked themselves. Modernized Japan was China's closest threat, but not her only one. Many others were just waiting for an excuse to push in.

Still, the court in Peking made one more desperate attempt to save the situation by changing its way of doing things. When it returned to the capital from its place of refuge in Sian, the empress dowager suddenly decided upon a dramatic move. It might be her only hope. She would reverse herself completely in her attitude toward foreigners and be gracious and friendly toward the ladies of the foreign diplomatic corps; she would issue decrees that would invite Western education and culture. She would throw China's doors wide open to all that was new. The diplomatic circle in Peking could scarcely believe it when they received cordial welcomes to the court. The foreign ladies regarded the dowager, who was nicknamed the Old Buddha, with mixed fear and suspicion. But they found that the changes were real and sweeping.

Reform

New schools to teach Western subjects were opened, and the old civil service system was abolished. The United States announced that part of the money due her from the indemnity connected with the Boxer Rebellion need not be paid, on condition that it be used to send Chinese students to the United States to study. China's new emphasis on modern education required new textbooks in Chinese. Publishing houses sprang up and began to produce books unlike any that China had ever seen.

Schools

Not only did the new China have to have new kinds of diplomatic relations, new schools, and new textbooks. It also needed a new and up-to-date Army. Military life had always been looked down on in China. Now military schools had to produce a new image of the officer and Army that the West, as well as China herself, would respect.

The Army

Reforms were pushed, as if to beat the march of history. Opium trade was still a serious problem. In 1906 the Chinese Government started a campaign to get rid of it entirely. Britain, under whose care most of the foreign trade in opium was being carried on, agreed to reduce the amount of opium which was imported into China by the same proportion as that which was being grown in China was cut back. The aim was to end opium trade in ten years.

Opium

The judicial system was overhauled, and many laws were changed, although extraterritoriality continued. There was

Law

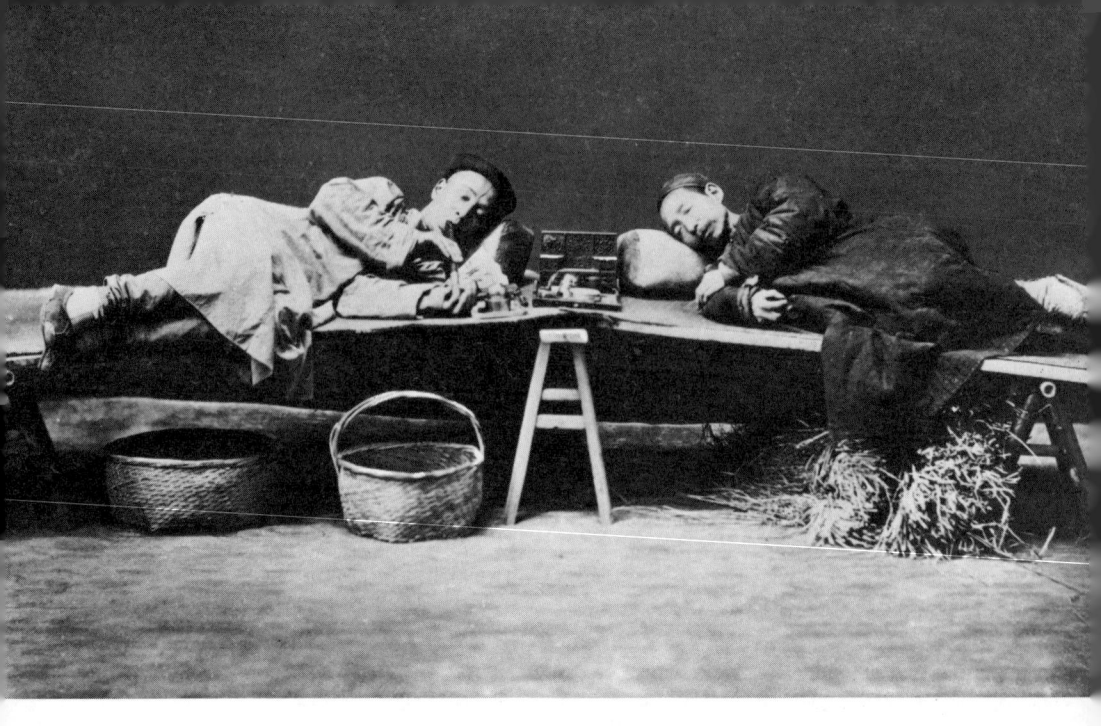

Opium smokers. Addiction to opium was one cause of wars between China and the West

talk of a better currency system. A special commission was set up to study constitutional government, some of its members going abroad for the purpose. The Peking Government promised to call a parliament with power to legislate by 1913.

Trade   Railroad and telegraph lines were extended and shipping increased. Foreign imports almost doubled between 1901 and 1911. Far inland, homes and shops used kerosene lamps and lanterns sold by the American Standard Oil Company of New York, instead of the bean oil lamps that they had used for centuries. Rich and poor alike began to smoke cigarettes of the British and American Tobacco Company, and they were soon caught by the habit. Japan found a boundless market for goods which she now manufactured much more cheaply than Western countries because of her low-paid workers.

Behind all the attempts to reform and change that were undertaken seriously by the Manchus in a desperate effort to catch up with time, revolution was brewing, unchecked by the government's effort. The effort had come too late to stop the ferment that was spreading all through the country. It was still hidden in secret societies, still talked about in undertones, but it had deep roots. It was alive and growing stronger, needing only to find its method.

The empress dowager and the emperor whom she had completely controlled died within a day of each other in 1908. The emperor's nephew, who was only two years old, was appointed to the throne. Real power was placed in the hands of a mediocre regent, and demands for more and more radical changes mushroomed. Young men whose eyes were flashing and whose faces were flushed with anger argued that the Manchus had to be dethroned, that the dynasty had to end.

The Regency

CHAPTER SEVEN

A Revolution That Failed

New horizons Thousands of young Chinese went to Japan to study after 1900, and hundreds sailed to Europe and the United States for the same purpose. When they came home, they usually found things just as they had been when they left and as they had been ever since they could remember. Manchu magistrates were still in charge of the local courts; masses of people were still following superstitious practices and were entirely ignorant of what was happening in the rest of the world. Most of them could not read, so how could they be informed?

Some of the returned students filled important positions in government, but many settled for any job that was well-paying and had prestige. Still others were determined to do everything they could to make their country assume her proper place in a modern world.

Missionaries were teaching ideas that were more revolutionary than they may have realized. They had come from countries where governments gave their citizens a voice, where women, as well as men, had rights. Moreover, they were preaching a gospel that would upset most socially accepted ideas anywhere if it was really followed. These ways of thinking could not avoid attracting aggressive and intelligent young people.

Western culture was exerting tremendous pressure on China. Although many of her young people were coming to the conclusion that change was going to have to come by a method that was much faster than reform, the best-known and most important revolutionist was Sun Yat-sen, one of the two young men who had taken a petition for change to Viceroy Li Hung-chang.

Sun Yat-sen Sun Yat-sen had done his high school work in Hawaii, because his elder brother, who was in business there, enrolled him in a mission school so that he would get a modern

A side street in Hong Kong. This was the city in which Sun Yat-sen joined the Christian church

education and learn English. Sun Yat-sen also learned about Christianity, to his brother's dismay. He sent the boy home as soon as he was graduated.

The young student was horrified at the ignorance and superstitution of the people in his native village near Canton in South China. He had forgotten that they were like this. He and a few of his friends scornfully broke some idols in a village temple one market day, when people had gathered there to burn incense and worship, and denounced the crowd in the temple courtyard. The village elders gathered and solemnly banished Sun Yat-sen from his home. This proved to be no punishment, because he wanted to get away. He

Sun Yat-sen's youth

went to Hong Kong, determined to continue his education.

In Hong Kong he again came into contact with Christianity through the friendship of an American missionary teacher. Sun Yat-sen joined the church and even went on preaching tours with his friend. When his brother in Hawaii discovered what he was doing, he sent for him. The two men quarrelled when they met again in Hawaii, and the elder brother refused the younger any more financial help when he found that his mind could not be changed. At this time, events in China were pushing Sun Yat-sen toward greater action to change his own country. It was 1885, and France had just defeated Chinese forces in a war in South China. The resulting treaty infuriated the young revolutionist.

Christians in Hawaii raised enough money for Sun Yat-sen to return to Hong Kong, on the promise that he would become a preacher. When he got back, however, he discovered that there was no theological school where he could get such training, so he turned to medicine. He could serve his people as a Christian doctor. After interruptions and delays, he secured a medical degree in 1892. It was two years after this that he and his close friend took their petition to Peking.

The Revive China Society After the failure in Peking, Sun Yat-sen returned to Hawaii, where he started a secret society of his own, calling it the Hsin Chung Hui, or Revive China Society. It was made up of a small group of overseas Chinese who were dedicated to the idea of modernizing their home country even if it had to be done by revolution.

When the war that had broken out between China and Japan in 1895 left China defeated and humiliated, and the Manchu Government in Peking started to talk about great reforms, Sun Yat-sen laid his own plans for revolution. Canton was the key spot for such an attempt, but the plot failed, and some of Sun's closest friends were executed. He escaped, but a price was put on his head, to stay there for many years. Reaching Japan, he had his hair, worn long in a queue, as all Chinese men were required to wear it at the command of the government, cut off, and he bought himself a Western-styled suit. He passed easily for a Japanese in such a disguise.

(*Left*) Dr Sun Yat-sen, leader of the Chinese revolution of 1911 and first President of the Chinese Republic.
(*Right*) Yuan Shih-k'ai, who replaced Sun Yat-sen as President only to lead it back toward monarchy

During the next five years Sun Yat-sen not only planned, but led attempt after attempt to overthrow the Manchu Government. Each one failed for some reason, such as a delay in the arrival of arms, deceit, trickery on the part of someone he trusted, or bad timing. He managed to escape with his life, but only narrowly. He was forever short of the money he needed for the revolution, and he made one world tour after another to get it. He worked through branches of the secret society that were gradually set up in many countries. The Hsin Chung Hui had forty branches in China alone by 1905. He reorganized the society into the T'ung Meng Hui, or Revolutionary Alliance, while he was in Japan in the same year. At this time he publicly stated his own political theory, the Three Principles of the People. The

Plots and counterplots

society started to publish its own monthly paper, and this was smuggled into China to encourage the revolutionary spirit there.

Sun Yat-sen had led or organized ten outbreaks against the Peking Government by 1911. All of them had failed. The latest one, that of April, 1911, resulted in the execution of seventy-two young men, who at once became famous as martyrs. A monument was later raised to them. The largest and most carefully planned of all revolutionary attempts was slated for October of the same year. It was to take place in Hankow, 650 miles up the Yangtze River from Shanghai. But a bomb exploded accidentally two days before the preparations were completed. The plot was discovered, and the revolution was on too soon. Sun Yat-sen was abroad, in the United States. When he reached Nanking in December, 1911, he was acclaimed provisional president of the new Chinese Republic, for the Manchu Government had resigned.

In a few weeks Sun Yat-sen, who was better as a leader of a revolution than as a political leader, stepped out of his position to give it to Yuan Shih-k'ai, who had been at the head of affairs in the capital during the emergency. This man was also the leader of the newly organized and modernized Chinese army in the north, but many knew him as no more than an old-fashioned warlord.

Yuan Shih-k'ai

Yuan Shih-k'ai did not understand or share Sun Yat-sen's dreams, nor did he even suspect the extent of the changes that the revolutionary leader had in mind. As time passed, it became clear that Yuan Shih-k'ai was interested only in strengthening his own political position and in putting his own favourites into office. He even dissolved the parliament and attacked the Kuomintang, or Nationalist Party, which had developed from the T'ung Meng Hui, or Revolutionary Alliance. The Kuomintang was the real organ of the new government, and to end it was to strike a blow at the heart of change. By 1915 Yuan Shih-k'ai was planning to reinstate the monarchy, with himself as emperor. Sun Yat-sen's revolution had failed again, but his dream of making China into a modern nation did not die so easily. In spite of all that Yuan Shih-k'ai could do, it was still very much alive.

CHAPTER EIGHT

China and the First World War

The great powers were so involved in Europe when the First World War broke out that they did not pay much attention to events in the Far East. Japan moved into German holdings in Shantung Province, because she had an alliance with Britain against Germany. She went even farther in January, 1915, by asking for many new rights in China. The Twenty-one Demands, as they were soon known, specified more concessions in Shantung Province, in south Manchuria, and in Inner Mongolia – rights to railroads and mining and joint control of China's most important iron mine and smelting company, to name only a few. In spite of bitter protest, President Yuan Shih-k'ai could not avoid granting some of the demands. In February and March, 1917, Japan went even farther and made a secret agreement with Britain, France, and Italy, which ensured that they would support her in demands which she intended to make at the peace table when the war ended.

The Twenty-one Demands

China did not take any part in the war until 1917 except to allow 175,000 of her workers, or coolies, to be recruited as labour battalions to work behind the lines in France, Iraq, and Africa. As the war continued, more and more pressure was put on China to take part in it on the side of the Allies. Yuan Shih-k'ai died in 1916, and the military men who were the leaders after his death argued about whether or not to enter the war. On 14 August 1917, China formally declared war on Germany, largely because she was promised a seat at the peace conference when the fighting was over. She counted on getting back some areas in foreign hands, especially those of Japan. China was now able, too, to take over German and Austrian concessions in her open ports, since these were enemy powers, and she was permitted to delay paying her Boxer indemnities to Allied powers.

Sun Yat-sen, who was in Canton at this time, knew that

China was in a desperate situation. He set up a military government there and had himself declared generalissimo, hoping to stabilize his group in the south and then begin to deal with the north. But this plan failed. He retired to Shanghai, where he had a small house in the French concession, guarded by French police.

The Peace   When the war ended, China was bitterly disappointed by the Treaty of Versailles, drawn up at the Paris Peace Conference, which ruled to let Japan keep Germany's former concessions in Shantung Province. When the news reached the Chinese people on 4 May 1919, thousands of students in Peking rose up in protest. Thirteen colleges and universities were represented in the demonstration, although it centred on Peking University. They marched to the palace gates, burned the house of the minister of state, whom they knew to be pro-Japanese, and beat the Chinese foreign minister. A great student strike began and spread to six other major cities. Some students were killed, and many others were wounded. Prisons were crowded.

Merchants joined in the student strike and closed their shops, because they handled a great deal of Japanese goods. The strike turned into a boycott of everything Japanese. Fights often broke out between Japanese people who were living in China and the local Chinese. Labour, which had only recently been organized in China, took part in mass demonstrations against Japan.

Growing unrest   As May moved into June, opposition to the Treaty of Versailles grew more intense, although the Chinese delegates to the peace conference had not signed it. New student organizations sprang up. One of the most important and longlived was the New Youth Society, of which Dr Hu Shih was a founder. China's feelings of nationalism had come to life in 1915 when Japan made her famous Twenty-one Demands. In 1917 Dr Hu Shih and other professors at Peking University had started a literary revolution. Stimulating new ideas began to be printed in everyday language instead of that of the old classics. Now in 1918, and continuing on, new magazines such as *New Youth* and *New Tide* appeared on the news stands. The study of socialism became popular.

Students were getting into China's politics for the first

time. They began to put their ideas of a new culture, a new science, and a new democracy into the anti-Manchu, anti-imperialist movement initiated by the revolutionists. Sun Yat-sen had talked to student groups around the world for many years, presenting them with ideas of change and representative government, but now, as the whole fabric of Chinese life was torn with change, he was scarcely involved in it. He seemed to be content to withdraw from the confusion, admiring a theory when action growing out of it was at hand. A visitor to his home in Shanghai reported that the only picture on the walls of his small, plainly furnished parlour was one of Abraham Lincoln.

The revolution started by the May Fourth Movement was so strong that the Chinese Communists claim it to have been the beginning of the revolutionary nationalism that led to their success.

CHAPTER NINE

The Nationalist Revolution

Young Chinese had become highly excited when the Russian Revolution took place in 1917, because it gave them great hopes of what might come about in their own country. A Chinese Communist Party was formed in 1921. Those who belonged to it could be members of the Kuomintang but were not permitted to serve as representatives of the Communist Party.

Two Governments Conditions in China were badly confused by this time. Two centres of government each claimed to head the republic. The Peking government was really in the hands of warlords, although it had a president. The Nationalist Party, the Kuomintang, headed a government in Canton, though it was actually under the control of a local clique. Because of the terrible state of affairs, Sun Yat-sen left Shanghai for Canton, determined to try once more to establish his government there. He got rid of the rival leaders and called the old parliament into session. In April, 1921, he was elected president.

The Canton government did not accept the government in Peking as authentic and declared Canton the national capital and Sun Yat-sen the national president. The republic proclaimed in this way really consisted of only the one province where Canton stood. Its governor was a general named Chen Chiung-ming. As president, Sun Yat-sen sent him out on campaigns into neighbouring provinces, in the hope of enlarging the republic. The general was successful in this, and Sun Yat-sen began to lay plans for him to go north to take Peking for the Nationalists of Canton. When General Chen refused to lead such an expedition, Dr Sun decided to do it himself. When General Chen deliberately ruined the expedition by sabotage, Dr Sun dismissed him from the governorship. This made him a bitter and dangerous enemy. He became so powerful that after a time he openly demanded that Sun Yat-sen resign from the presidency. In the summer of 1922 General Chen arranged for an attack on the presidential mansion in Canton, with the intention of capturing the president. Dr and Madame Sun barely managed to escape with their lives and took refuge on a small Chinese gunboat on the nearby river. They reached Shanghai only after many hairbreadth dangers.

The United States had called the Washington Conference in 1921 and had asked China to lay her problems before the world there. A Nine-Power Treaty had resulted, in which the United States had proposed that foreign nations give up their special privileges in China and act together, instead of each for itself, in all that they undertook in that country – a way of restating the Open Door Policy. The proposal helped China in her foreign relations in a general way, but conditions in the country were so bad and the government so divided that something much more crucial was needed. *The Washington Conference*

Dr Sun knew by now that he did not have the ability to make a military success out of the revolution. He had to have expert help for this, and the best source of such help seemed to be Russia, which was ready to give it. He began to reorganize the Kuomintang, patterning it after the Russian Soviet, or Socialist, Council, with the help of Adolf Joffe, a Russian adviser, who was in Shanghai. They made a public statement together, in which they declared that Russia was going to support the Chinese Revolution.

The first immediate need was for military strength. In 1923 Dr Sun sent one of his young generals named Chiang Kai-shek to Moscow to study military methods. When he returned, Russia sent some of her own advisers back with him. These men helped to set up the Whampoa Military Academy, not far from Canton. Michael Borodin, a clever and widely experienced man, was one of the outstanding Russians who came to China at this time. He was also a representative of the Russian international organization, the Comintern. He became the Kuomintang expert on how to set up revolutions. Now that China had turned toward Russia, money and arms began to pour in from there. *Need for military strength*

The Chinese Communist Party was still insignificant. It had only 300 members in 1922, as compared with a membership of 150,000 in the Kuomintang. By 1925 the Communist

Party still had only about 1,500 members and was not officially represented in the Kuomintang.

In 1924 the government in Peking elected a new president. Bribes were used so openly that rival warlord groups protested the election. A general named Wu P'ei-fu was connected with the affair. Dr Sun made a public statement to the effect that he was going north to put an end to the militarism and imperialism there, draw up new and just treaties, and establish new laws. General Wu P'ei-fu was naturally his target.

Feng Yu-hsiang

Before Sun Yat-sen could even get started, another man named General Feng Yu-hsiang, who called himself the Christian General because he had joined a church, seized Peking. He made Wu P'ei-fu retreat hastily and before General Chang Tso-lin, the man whom Sun Yat-sen was counting on for help, could take over the city, he had full control of it himself. Now Feng Yu-hsiang declared that the north and the south were going to unite. He said that a conference for this purpose was being called, and he sent Dr Sun an invitation to attend it. It seemed to Dr Sun that he would have to accept, for now the group he favoured was back in control of Peking. Even Michael Borodin urged him to go to celebrate the unification of China. It was particularly important for Sun Yat-sen to go to Peking, too, because China and Russia had come to an agreement about their diplomatic relationship. The first foreign diplomatic representative with the rank of ambassador ever to be stationed in Peking was the Russian Lev Mikhailovich Karakhan. He was automatically the senior foreign officer and, thus, chief of the foreign legations.

Sun Yat-sen accepted the invitation to the unification conference, even though he had not been well for a long time. He scheduled speeches in Hong Kong, Shanghai, and other coastal cities in China and Japan, where his ship would dock along his route. On these occasions he spoke out strongly and bitterly against Britain, other European countries, and the United States. He announced his own plans for reorganization once the government was unified, for he did not doubt that he would be president. But as he went on his way he began to hear strange whispers to the effect that the government in Peking was going ahead without waiting for his arrival. He began to suspect that the invitation he had received was only a farcical courtesy and that he was being double-crossed. When he got as far as Tientsin, he suddenly collapsed with illness, and when, after a few days of rest, he started on again, everyone knew that he was terribly ill. He died in Peking on 12 March 1925.

Death of Sun Yat-sen

General Chiang Kai-shek was at the head of the Nationalist forces, so he was clearly the one to undertake the expedition to Peking that was to bring the whole country under one flag. By now he had grown suspicious of Communist propaganda because of its ability to win the loyalty of the country people. Students and workers, too, seemed to accept Communist ideas readily. General Chiang was on the point of making up his mind to rid the country of Communists altogether. In the spring of 1926 he authorized a coup against the Communists in Canton.

General Chiang started the Northern Expedition from Canton toward Peking in the winter of 1926–7. Everything went well as far as Wuchang, near Hankow, which fell on 10 October 1926. The Nationalist Government in Canton moved to Hankow and set itself up there. General Chiang was delayed by major resistance in Nanchang, to the south. Victorious there, he moved directly eastward toward Shanghai. The Nationalist Government from Canton followed him and set itself up in Hankow. Britain organized an international force of 40,000 men to protect Shanghai if

The approach to the tomb of Sun Yat-sen on Purple Mountain, Nanking

this should become necessary while the Northern Expedition was going on. Missionaries and foreign traders from the interior of China were pouring into the coastal city for refuge, because they expected disorder.

General Chiang

In March, 1927, General Chiang's troops reached Nanking. He had decided to strengthen his position by seizing the rich Yangtze Valley instead of going on toward Peking from Hankow. Now some of his men got entirely out of hand and attacked foreigners and looted university and hospital buildings in Nanking. Some foreigners were killed, and many institutions were emptied of everything that they had contained. Foreign gunboats anchored in the river under treaty rights shelled the city to stop the pillaging and then evacuated their nationals to Shanghai.

General Chiang had sent organizers ahead to prepare Shanghai for his arrival. He took over the city easily and then turned on those who had worked for him, betraying them. While he had appeared to be getting the city ready for a Nationalist régime, in the way Dr Sun Yat-sen had intended, he had really abandoned that for the help he could get from rich, but conservative bankers and businessmen. He ordered a purge of the labour unions and of all who might not come to his support now that he was going to reject any further cooperation with Russia. He had been getting more and more uneasy about Communist power, because, now that the Chinese Revolution had failed, Soviet ideas were spreading and growing stronger every day. Chinese Communist leaders were able to adapt Russian programmes to local situations, improving life for the poor, who had nothing to lose, anyway. The Communist ideal was quietly spreading among millions of people who had suffered injustice at the hands of warlords and landlords for centuries. It was leading them on like a bright star in a dark sky.

Nanking

General Chiang set up his Nationalist capital, not in Peking or Canton, but in Nanking, as Dr Sun had always planned, in April, 1927. Hankow was also under his control, for the liberal group that had moved there from Canton had broken apart. The Nationalist Government expelled all Communists from the Kuomintang and then began campaigns to destroy them altogether. Small Communist groups down in Canton tried repeatedly to take control of that city but did not succeed. After they had failed many times they set up their government, or soviet, in the mountains of Kiangsi Province, south of the Yangtze River. This government was headed by Mao Tse-tung; Chou En-lai was another important leader. Both of these men were to become world-famous.

General Chiang continued to organize the government in Nanking. It was officially recognized as the authentic government of China by most foreign countries. Steps were taken to end the unequal treaties against China. Nanking itself was modernized; a permanent grave for Dr Sun Yat-sen was built against the side of famous Purple Mountain outside the city, and the diplomats of other countries moved their legations from Peking to Nanking. Everything looked promising for the new régime.

General Chiang took up the Northern Expedition again in the spring of 1928. He officially occupied Peking in June and changed the name to Peiping, or Northern Peace, from Peking, or Northern Capital. Even Manchuria, which was under the leadership of Chang Hsueh-liang, or the Young Marshal – the son of old Chang Tso-lin – recognized the Nationalist Government. General Chiang Kai-shek must have felt that Dr Sun's dream had at last come true. All of China proper was under the white sun of the Kuomintang flag. Two major worries remained. One was Russia's too great interest in China; the other was the fact that campaigns against the Communists always failed.

Peiping

CHAPTER TEN

General Chiang Kai-shek and the New Capital

All hope for the new government centred on General Chiang Kai-shek, the son of a merchant who had lived in a village near Ningpo on the East China Sea, not far from Shanghai. General Chiang had been fascinated by military heroes and stories of military life from the time he was a small boy. After he had finished high school, he spent a year at China's first military academy in Paoting, near Peking, preparing to enter the Tokyo Military Staff College for training as an officer. Following his graduation, the Peking Government assigned him to the Japanese Army for two years.

Chiang's aims   Chiang Kai-shek had had a chance to get acquainted with Sun Yat-sen, who was then in Japan, and joined his secret society in 1910. He soon became involved in some of the first revolutionary activities in Shanghai. Through Dr Sun, he got to know the Soong family, which was at that time living in Shanghai, but he was not deeply drawn into the Chinese Revolution until Dr Sun sent him to Moscow to study military tactics in 1923. From that time on, he considered himself a real revolutionist, convincing Dr Sun that a strong military force was absolutely necessary and demonstrating his own ability as a military leader. While he accepted the goals of the Kuomintang and, in his own way, tried to further them and protect them, he did not really understand democratic methods nor did he sympathize with the belief that poor, ordinary people might have dreams or should have rights. He was unable to put himself in their place.

When General Chiang enlisted the help of powerful businessmen in Shanghai, had the city prepared for his taking it over then purged the labour unions and got rid of all who could be called Communist or even liberal, he sincerely thought that these moves were necessary. He really believed that they were the only way to establish the Nationalist

Government securely, even though these severe steps might deny such principles as the rights of the people whom the revolution was supposed to be defending.

General Chiang took a beautiful new wife with him to Nanking when he set up the Nationalist Government there in April, 1927. She was Soong Mayling, a graduate of Wellesley College in America, the third daughter of the Soong family, with whom he had become acquainted in Shanghai. Her grace and her fluency in English, a language that he had never learned, were to help him in many ways when foreign leaders and diplomats came to the new capital. Nanking was soon the most modern capital China had ever had, a suitable government centre in keeping with the dignity of a twentieth-century Middle Kingdom.

Between 1927 and 1937 General Chiang Kai-shek was a successful leader. The government was established and began to move through the three stages Dr Sun Yat-sen had outlined for it. The first of these was that of unification by military means; the second, that of political development under the Kuomintang; the third was that of getting a constitutional democracy started. The military stage seemed to be completed. General Chiang announced that the second stage, that of political development under the Kuomintang, was beginning. The party and its Central Executive Committee held full power. They chose all the high officials and made all the important decisions. This meant that the country was really under a party dictatorship.

Chiang's success

The Nationalist Government now wanted to free itself of extraterritoriality and foreign concessions won by treaties in the past. The Washington Conference, which had been called in 1921, had taken some steps in this direction. Now further progress resulted from the fact that diplomats from abroad reported favourably to their home countries about the Chinese government's stability. The capital was beginning to glisten with modernization and to hum with efficiency. The dignified general who stood at the head of the government and his beautiful wife inspired confidence. In 1927 General Chiang had begun strengthening his military organization by inviting German advisers to come to Nanking. There were more than thirty there by 1935.

For ten years the Kuomintang was successful, although

during this time General Chiang still had to put down old enemies from time to time. Warlords in the north joined together under the leadership of Feng Yu-hsiang and moved against General Chiang's forces, but they were defeated. Although the government group that had centred in Hankow withdrew to Canton and dissolved there, neighbouring provinces in the south staged a rebellion against Nanking's authority, which was stopped only with difficulty.

Communist opposition

General Chiang succeeded in controlling all opposition except that of the Communists. Nothing really stopped them, because they were able to build up a powerful following of young men who believed that General Chiang was only another warlord in new dress, and of deserters from the Nationalists. Supplies of arms came from their successful engagements with the enemy, from deserters, through the black market, and from their own primitive munitions plants, which were hidden in the mountains. They held scattered areas of land, where they established miniature communal societies, or soviets. By 1930 the Red Army was no longer small or disorganized. It was a military power to be feared. The soviets in four provinces were no longer small either. Though they appeared to be nothing more than communities, they were really strong centres of political propaganda and authority. The most important of these centres was the one in Juichin, Kiangsi Province.

General Chiang was certain that the Communist network was his government's greatest danger. He launched attack after attack against the Communists between 1930 and 1933, but all of them failed, because the enemy melted away under the seemingly irresistible impact of his well-disciplined troops. He heard reports that some of these well-disciplined troops were going over to the Communists in large numbers.

Russian influence

Nanking and Moscow were no longer on friendly terms because of General Chiang's break with the liberal Nationalist group. Russia had been exerting her influence in borderlands, like Outer Mongolia and Sinkiang Province, to infringe on China. She would have gone farther if her fear of Japan had not checked her, for she would always stand with China against Japan, their common enemy. But the Chinese Eastern Railway, which ran north and south through Manchuria and was jointly operated by Russians and Chinese, caused trouble. The Young Marshal, son of Chang Tso-lin whom Dr Sun had championed in his fatal trip north, suspected that the Russians were planning to take full control of the railroad. His men raided the railway offices and arrested some of the Russian officers because of papers that were discovered. Russia responded by sending in troops, thereby worsening relations.

Japan's interest in China, like that of Russia, centred in North China. She already controlled a large part of Manchuria because of railroads she had built there and because of her lease on the Liaotung Peninsula. She needed both space and resources, because her population was increasing so rapidly.

Japan

General Chiang kept an anxious eye on Japan. Some of his men began to come right out and beg him to check Japan before it was too late to stop her encroachment in the north. He refused to take such steps, counting on the loyalty and strength of the Young Marshal to handle the situation there with his own strong Manchurian troops. General Chiang was still more afraid of the Reds than he was of Japan. Although he knew that Japan was clever, she fought with outright military forces, while the Communists organized themselves underground and fought with guerrillas. He kept on doggedly sending one expedition after another to exterminate the Reds, sometimes even leading an expedition himself, but he could not get a clear victory.

While General Chiang was busy with the Reds, Japan suddenly seized the Manchurian city, Mukden, in September, 1931, claiming that four of her citizens, including a military officer, had been arrested in a restricted military zone. General Chiang had warned the Young Marshal to be especially careful to avoid any clash with the Japanese. Now Japan used this incident as a pretext to encourage the Chinese who were living in Manchuria to set up a new state of their own. She organized this gradually, and in 1932 she introduced it to the world as Manchukuo, or the country of the Manchus. Although this state was completely under Japan's power, it went through the form of declaring itself independent. Manchukuo was a splendid prize because one-fifth of all of China's trade was carried on there. Its port city, Dairen, was next to Shanghai in importance. Japan knew the fine

Manchurian Incident

RUSSIA
Amur River
HEILUNGKIANG
OUTER MONGOLIA
Harbin
KIRIN
MANCHUKUO
LIAONING
CHAHAR
JEHOL
Mukden
INNER MONGOLIA
NINGHSIA
SUIYUAN
Kalgan
PEKING (Peiping)
Tientsin
Taku
Paoting
HOPEI
KOREA
Yellow R.
KANSU
SHANSI
Tsingtao
Tsinan
SHANTUNG
KOKONOR

Hsuchow
HONAN
KIANGSU
Sian
(Hsianfu)
Nanking
Shanghai
HUPEH
ANHUI
Ya-lung
R.
HSIK'ANG
SZECHWAN
Yangtze
R.
Ichang
Hankow
Wuchang
Hangchow
Hanyang
(Wuhan)
Ningpo
Chikow
CHEKIANG
Chungking
Tatu R.
Changsha
Nanchang
KIANGSI
Wenchow
HUNAN
Juichin
FUKIEN
KWEICHOW
Foochow
Mekong
BURMA ROAD
Kunming
(Yunnanfu)
Taipei
TAIWAN
(To Ledo,
Stilwell Road,
"The Hump")
YUNNAN
KWANGSI
KWANGTUNG
Canton
Waichow
River
Hong Kong
Lashio
BURMA
(To Rangoon)
FRENCH
INDO-
CHINA
South China Sea
SIAM
HAINAN
Route of
"THE LONG MARCH"
0 50 100 150 300
Scale of Miles
Don Pitcher

The Lytton Commission

possibilities it offered for industrial development. It had not only coal and oil, but rich soil and a seacoast.

General Chiang realized that his armies could not match the well-trained Japanese forces. He had seen them firsthand years before. Now, in desperation, China took her case to the League of Nations, although it was still a very new organization. The League protested against Japan's behaviour and then appointed a commission to investigate what was going on in Manchuria. When the Lytton Commission reported its findings, Japan reacted by declaring that she was going to withdraw from the League of Nations. The United States reasoned with Japan without success and refused to recognize the state of Manchukuo.

Disasters

For a number of reasons 1931 was an especially bad year for the Chinese capital. Campaigns against the Communists continued to fail; a terrible flood swept down through the Yangtze Valley; Japan invaded the north. The apex of the flood was in Wuhan where three cities, Hanyang, Hankow, and Wuchang, stand. River tributaries burst dikes and dams, flooded the countryside, and rushed into city streets. Starvation and epidemics followed. Hundreds of thousands of people lost their lives because of the floods. Nanking tried to take relief measures, but nothing could be effective in the widespread situation. Besides, there were many reports of food hoarders and of officials who grew richer from funds intended to help those who had lost everything. The great flood of 1931 did not win friends for the Nanking Government.

The situation was so desperate that people said that General Chiang would surely rally all forces against Japan. It was already clear that that country had her eye on Jehol, another northern province, and that she was thinking about possibilities in the Yangtze Valley, too. But General Chiang still waited.

In 1932 Japan boldly attacked Shanghai and bombed a large part of the city. Chinese forces fought her so bravely that the world acclaimed their action, even though, in the end, they had to withdraw. The League of Nations now intervened on China's behalf in the settlements that followed the war, but Japan had, just the same, succeeded in forcing open a door into the Yangtze Valley for herself. This valley was China's garden spot, her main trade route, and the waterway connecting her most modern cities with the great inland.

China's economy grew worse with every defeat and with every new effort to unify by wiping out the Communists. War was wasting her resources, no matter against whom it was fought. War delayed, too, the modernization that was so crucially needed. Many Chinese who saw this began to lose sympathy for the party dictatorship, which was centered in General Chiang. In spite of this rising mood of criticism, he still stubbornly insisted that the country had to be unified before it could throw itself against Japan.

He sometimes wondered secretly why he could not inspire his troops with the kind of devotion and courage that the Communists had. It was this spirit that made it almost impossible to defeat their guerrillas. They appeared to actually believe in their cause and hope for a new kind of government and subsequently a new life. He heard that even the poorest country fellow was heartened when he saw that the Red soldiers were poor, cold, underfed, and often in great danger and yet did not mistreat or steal from those who quartered them and shared what they had. *Chiang's leadership*

Madame Chiang had lived in the United States long enough to catch some of the idealism to be found there, and she could understand better than her husband why the Communists were so successful. She wanted to find a way of stirring the people to support the Nationalist programme, and at last she and the General together thought of a plan that might inspire enthusiasm. They called it the New Life Movement and started it in 1934. It was intended to build up self-respect and to introduce gradually a better social system. Announcements and posters flooded the provinces, and enforcement of the announced rules followed. Everyone seemed to conform, at first, even though they might be grumbling to themselves. People tidied the streets and markets, buttoned their clothes more carefully, and did not lounge in the heat of the afternoon, as they liked to do. But the programme did not touch the roots of the problem. It did not promise to change the causes of poverty, stop injustices, or check graft. The sprucing-up did not last long. *The New Life Movement*

While the New Life Movement was being put into action,

the Chinese soviets that were scattered around the country grew stronger, because they were supported by the local people. Cooperatives were producing more and more goods for their own use, while print shops turned out masses of propaganda. Juichin continued to be the centre of the soviet organization, with Mao Tse-tung, Chou En-lai, and a man named Chu Teh, the leaders.

Chiang's noose

When General Chiang failed in wiping out the power of the Communists, he consulted with his German advisers about a new strategy, a blockade that would encircle the main Communist stronghold in Kiangsi. A chain of pillboxes and fortresses joined by highways would be constructed around the whole area and manned by guards. When the right time came, the encirclement would begin to strangle the Communist group. Such a huge plan required large sums of money and the labour of thousands of men, but it was begun.

The Chinese Communists had been keeping in touch with Moscow, although their situation was very unlike that of Russia, where Communist activity had first been concentrated in the cities. China was really rural, and the largest proportion of the people who were demanding a better life were peasants and farmers, rather than industrial workers. They could fight much more successfully as guerrillas than as soldiers in formal battles, because they were used to physical work and knew every inch of the landscape.

But when General Chiang's plan was near completion, 100,000 Communists were encircled and about to be strangled economically and militarily. They turned to Moscow for advice in the emergency, and on the basis of the advice they received, they divided into five sections, and on a night in October, 1934, they managed to slip through the noose of the blockade by the thousand. It would not have been possible to do this without the strong support of the local people. In some instances, these people replaced them in the blockaded area so that they would not be missed and suspicions would not be aroused. The plan succeeded, even though it seemed like a miracle.

The Communists had decided upon Yenan, Shensi Province, as their destination. It lay in Western China, 6,000 miles away, where another 10,000 Communists had gathered. These would be awaiting the arrival of the Kiangsi

Communists, who were setting out on what was soon called the Long March. Twenty thousand of the 90,000 who began to move north and then west, survived the wars that had to be fought along the way, the strafing by General Chiang's Air Force, the hazards of high, snow-covered mountains and deep river gorges with tricky currents, as well as hunger and disease.

The Long March

It was clear that the Communists had not been exterminated, even though General Chiang had encircled them, even though he had 700,000 men under arms to their 150,000 ragtag guerrillas. But he had succeeded in pushing them into an out-of-the-way corner, where they could no longer be a threat to the Nanking government. He stationed the Young Marshal, who was now deputy commander in chief for bandit suppression for three provinces, in Sian, the capital of Shensi Province, in the northwestern part of which the Communists were now located, and put him in charge of watching them. They had made Yenan, a town located in the mountains about 100 miles from the Great Wall, their capital. Centuries ago, nomadic raiders and then Genghis Khan's hordes had thundered into China on their way to Sian at this very point.

CHAPTER ELEVEN

Incident at Sian

The Japanese threat   Japan was now the greatest threat to the Nationalist Government. Russia hoped that all forces would join to resist her, because this might keep her from moving into Russian-held areas in North China; the Communists wanted this because it would distract Nanking's attention from what they themselves were doing. In August, 1935, the Communists took the initiative and called on the Nationalists to join them in all-out resistance to Japan, but General Chiang did not pay any attention to their proposal.

Many of the Young Marshal's troops were from Manchuria, and they were getting homesick. They had no real heart for suppressing any but the Japanese bandits, as they labelled those who were a threat under their assignment of bandit suppression. The Young Marshal was more and more worried about what Japan might be planning to do, because the government in Tokyo had recently fallen into the hands of a militaristic group that wanted to take a more openly aggressive line toward China.

General Chiang found out that opposition to Nanking's policy was increasing in Canton and quickly checked it by making a financial arrangement with the opposition leaders there. The truth was that his attitude was strongly condemned, not only in the south, but throughout the nation. He was still depending on the advice of the Germans, but though they were highly professional, they were also strongly conservative. Time passed, and still General Chiang paid no attention to what he heard around him. In the same way, he appeared to overlook the rebellions against his policy that broke out in first one place and then another. His most dangerous failing was that he did not take into account the *Nationalism*   spirit of nationalism that was springing up strongly all through the country. It would have been a source of great power for his cause if he had recognized it and made use of it.

The Communists in the northwest had established a second base a little to the north of Yenan, in a place called Paoan. They made secret contact with the Young Marshal in Sian in the spring of 1936. As this contact grew, some of the Communist leaders went to live in Sian as representatives of their group. During the same period, General Chiang's German advisers decided that he ought to plan yet another, the sixth anti-Communist campaign. He accepted the idea, sure that this time he would be able to crush the enemy completely; it would also give the Young Marshal's men something to do.

But General Chiang did not have the slightest idea that many of the Young Marshal's men had already gone over to the Communist side. Nor did he realize how quickly the Communist forces were growing. Two warlords and their large armies had joined them, so that by the autumn of 1936 there were about 80,000 Communist regulars, almost as many as had set out on the Long March two years earlier, although not all of them were armed.

In October General Chiang went to Sian to talk over his plans for the sixth anti-Communist campaign with the Young Marshal. He was astonished to have that young man propose, as the Communists had in the summer of 1935, that the war between the two groups be altogether halted and that, instead, they join and make an alliance with Russia against Japan. General Chiang was tired of pressure on this point; he turned the proposal down harshly and left Sian. Even though he was facing discouragements, he would not consider giving up his plan to annihilate the Reds through this new campaign against them. It was already scheduled to begin on 12 December.

The Young Marshal called a meeting of his men on 11 December and they came to a quick decision as to what they would have to do. The next day they arrested General Chiang Kai-shek, who had put up at a mountain resort nearby, protected only by his bodyguard. The Young Marshal then sent out an open telegram addressed to Nanking, but informing the nation, as well as that city, that General Chiang would have to accept eight points before he would be released. These points amounted to an agreement that the civil war would be stopped at once so that all forces

Arrest of Chiang Kai-shek

could join against the Japanese aggressors and that the government would be reorganized, uniting the Communists and the Nationalists.

Panic Nanking went into a state of panic over the dramatic kidnapping. The minister of war immediately planned a punitive expedition by air, without stopping to think of what might happen to General Chiang in Sian, where he was under arrest, if that city were bombed. Some of the most extreme Communists in Sian, on the other hand, suggested that the best thing to do was simply to execute their captive.

The strange situation turned into a kind of game between the politicians on both sides, for each saw a chance for clever playing to its own advantage. After several days of bickering, it was actually the Communist leaders, who still had contact with the Comintern, who saved General Chiang. They saw that the eight points which the Sian group were demanding that he accept could be of great help to the Communists, because they would involve the Nationalists and so broaden possibilities and share burdens. Some of them went to Sian to help the Young Marshal persuade General Chiang to agree to the proposals, among them Chou En-lai.

The Young Marshal was miserably unhappy about the whole kidnapping episode, because General and Madame Chiang were really his friends, but he knew of no other way to force the General to agree to oppose Japan before it was too late. During the days that he was under arrest, the General would not speak to the Young Marshal or touch the special food and drink that he brought. General Chiang lay in bed, his face turned to the wall, silent except for curt reprimands, which he snapped out from time to time.

A truce Madame Chiang managed to arrange a truce that would keep Nanking from bombing Sian for a time and then flew to the northern city herself, accompanied by her Australian adviser, William Henry Donald, determined to get talks started. Finally, on 24 December, without actually signing any papers, General Chiang agreed to join his forces with those of the Communists against Japan, ending the civil war. He was flown back to Nanking on Christmas Day, and the city went wild with relief. The triumphal return made it seem as though he had been the winner, especially since the

Young Marshal, under invisible arrest, was a member of the party. In January the Young Marshal was tried and sentenced to ten years' imprisonment, after which he was to be given a special pardon. He would be required to live under the watchful eye of the General for the rest of his life, and this he is still doing.

In spite of, perhaps partly because of, the incident in Sian, General Chiang Kai-shek had reached the highest point of his career so far. He stood as a symbol of China's unified resistance to Japan. While he went through the formalities of resigning his position because of what he termed his failures, the resignation was quickly rejected by the Nationalist Government.

The hero

CHAPTER TWELVE

The Great Migration: Free China

The Executive Committee of the Kuomintang met for the first time after the kidnapping in February, 1937. It received a telegram from the Central Committee of the Communists, which pledged that if the Nationalists would agree to stop all civil war and concentrate on resisting Japan, the Communists would stop all their military activities against the Nationalists, change their soviets into special area governments of the Chinese Republic, and their Red Army into the Chinese National Revolutionary Army, under Nanking's authority. A series of meetings between the two Chinese groups was planned for the coming summer, when all these matters could be discussed between representatives of both Nationalists and Communists.

Japanese policy

When Japan found out that the Communists were proposing unity, she reacted strongly against it and did everything she could to check any such coalition of Chinese forces, because she had hoped for an alliance with the Nationalists against Russia. Now Japan quickly proposed and pressed for economic cooperation between Manchukuo and Nanking and herself, as well as a military pact between the three parties against the Communists. But the Nationalist Government knew that to accept such a plan meant that Japan would lead it, that China would have to give up her independence to come under Japan's growing authority and ambition.

Beginning of Second Chino-Japanese War

On 7 July an incident took place between Japanese troops, who were on manœuvres, and Chinese soldiers stationed at Lukouchiao, also known as the Marco Polo Bridge, at Wanping, a town near Peiping. The Japanese claimed that they were looking for one of their men; the Chinese in charge refused to let them enter the walled town to search for him. Local people thought it was just a small affair that could be settled easily. But the incident was an excuse for

Japan to start much larger hostilities against China, and the settlement that was reached soon broke down. War between Japan and China began. Japanese forces advanced from Tientsin toward Peiping and were soon bombing the famous Western Hills near the old capital. On 8 August they occupied the city. The new coalition Chinese Government that had just been worked out had assured the people that they would not be asked to evacuate areas for military action, but now thousands abandoned their homes and fields to escape the Japanese invaders. It was scarcely necessary for a formal announcement of the Chinese united front to be made, since the outbreak of the war left no alternative, but the statement was broadcast.

The country had come to a new time and situation. War-lords, who had only a few years earlier divided the loyalties of the people, were almost all gone now, and the threat to China was clear – Japanese imperialism. The Chinese as a whole were drawn together in the new experience of being one political group, rather than just one culture or one civilization, as they had been for such a long time. The sense of nationalism that had been developing rapidly now suddenly loomed strong and demanding.

Chinese unity

The Chinese Communists hoped that their country would be able to save herself because of this national feeling. They believed that the political leadership that tapped it most successfully would win. Nationalists, on the other hand, were only cooperating with the Communists because they had to, still unaware of how thinking across the country had changed. Their leadership had not kept up with the times.

War against China could not possibly be waged on the large scale it was now assuming without attracting the attention of the rest of the world. Too many foreign nations had interests in both trade and missions in the Far East. The United States protested against what Japan was doing, and quarantining was suggested, but no action was taken. American manufacturers continued to send scrap iron to Japan, as they had been doing. The United States kept to her policy of not intervening in China's affairs and did not offer help. Germany had been giving Nanking military advice, and now she attempted to mediate between the two warring countries through her ambassadors. Japan who was allied with Germany by a pact against Russia, rejected any conciliation and demanded that the military advisers which the Nationalist government was using be sent home.

Japan and Russia were the two outside powers who had the biggest fight over China. Neither believed that China was going to be strong enough as a combatant to protect herself. Moreover, Russia had a peculiar relationship with China, because she had signed a nonaggression pact with her at about the time the united front was declared. This provided China with thousands of tons of war goods in exchange for Chinese tungsten, tea, and wool. The arms and raw goods were transported either way laboriously by overland routes. As time went on, Russia would send China planes and pilots, too. Russian advisers gradually replaced the Germans who left, but General Chiang used them so little that they did not stay.

Japanese victories As the war went on, Japan won almost every engagement, moving steadily westward in the north, always with a wary eye on Russia. She took over cities that gave her an entrance into Shansi Province and kept on into the next province, Suiyuan, occupying its capital. She set up what purported to be an independent government there.

In the meantime, the Chinese had established a strong line of defence between Paoting and Peiping. When the Japanese turned southward in a two-pronged attack on the Nationalist general, who held that position with 50,000 men, the Chinese withdrew to Paoting for fear of being encircled. Although they put up a desperate resistance there, the city fell to the Japanese in September. This made it possible for them to move southward rapidly into Shansi Province from a new direction. They defeated a Communist force that opposed them and took Taiyüan, the capital, in November. Another line of march from Tientsin was started almost at once and moved into Shantung Province.

Japan was also getting into China at other points. During the summer of 1937 she had attacked Shanghai and had been astonished at how strongly she was opposed. But the Chinese had to retreat when the Japanese made a surprise landing at Hangchow and attacked their flank. The retreat meant that the way to Nanking lay open, and Japanese forces began a steady advance up the river valley, toward the capital. The

Nanking Government, knowing that the enemy's relentless movement could not be stopped, announced that it was going inland.

More than the government was moving. Industries and munitions plants had already been dismantled and taken inland by boat, by train, or carried on the backs of men, to be set up again in far interior places and begun to produce as well as they could. Students, too, moved away from the coast, often travelling long distances on foot, holding classes wherever they stopped – perhaps in temples or perhaps just in the open. Not only were these students escaping from the Japanese; they were indirectly playing an important role in China's future because of the influence they had on the people living in isolated areas. Some local leaders of the villages that the students reached had already gone over to the Japanese out of fear, or they had escaped. Now young intellectuals who were strong and full of determination to resist took their places. Some college professors from Peiping who still remembered the May 4 Incident and others who had taken part when the students protested about the Treaty of Versailles now became guerrilla leaders. Still other college men stayed out of politics and threw themselves into making their institutions in exile new centres of modern education.

In the north and south these migrant patriots became the heroes of a new Chinese folklore. They had to live as frugally as the common people around them did; they had to share what little they had; they had to be enormously courageous. Because of all these things, they appealed to the imagination, just as characters out of the past did.

The Japanese occupied Nanking in December, 1937. Their troops looted the city and treated the citizens with great brutality and were condemned by nations across the world for their behaviour. The occupation came to be known as one of the worst in history's records.

After capturing Nanking, Japan turned toward Canton. She sent in 30,000 men from the coast, supported by naval craft on the nearby Pearl River, and the city could not resist for long. The fall of Canton ended Japan's Shanghai-Nanking-Canton campaign. Now she concentrated again on Shantung Province in the northeast, where China's resistance was strong. Tsinan, the capital, was taken, but only after

Chinese withdrawal

Occupation of Nanking

The Battle of Taierchwang bitter fighting, and the Japanese then centred on the important city of Hsuchow. At first the Chinese held firm. Fighting was concentrated on Taierchwang, a small town outside the city. Just when the Japanese thought that they were getting control of it, they found themselves trapped. They were badly defeated in what turned into a dramatic victory for the Chinese Armies, and all China celebrated the event. The Battle of Taierchwang became famous at once.

But this was only a small delay for Japan. She sent in forces from two directions now and, cutting the railway that made Hsuchow important, took the city in the spring. Most of the Chinese escaped westward, pursued by the enemy. As the battle grew more bitter, the Chinese began to set fire to the countryside as they had to abandon it – the scorched earth policy that left nothing for the enemy. They also broke the dikes of the Yellow River to flood the countryside and impede the progress of the Japanese. These ancient dikes were the only protection the people had against floods, because the river bottom had gradually silted up to a level higher than that of the surrounding fields. The entire area was soon under water. It was never possible to estimate how many people lost their lives, but such a protest went up that Nanking tried hard to find some way of justifying her action, although it was clearly a desperate Chinese move that forced Japan to change her plans. She now began to concentrate her attacks along the Yangtze, instead of in the north.

Japan advances Cities in the Yangtze Valley fell to Japan in quick succession during the summer of 1938. All that slowed the invasion was the terrible summer heat, which the Japanese were not used to, and epidemic diseases. Hankow, Wuchang and Hanyang fell in October. The Japanese pushed on toward Yoyang gateway to the rich province of Hunan and its capital, Changsha. Chinese troops set fire to the city in panic when they heard a rumour that the enemy was only a few miles away, but the Japanese had stopped short of it.

Chungking The Nanking government had moved by stages to the inland city of Chungking. Chungking was now thought of as the capital of Free China. Years before, when General Chiang had flown over the city, he had made a mental note of the fact that it was located in such a way that it could be well-protected from any but air attacks. He had suspected that the government was going to be pushed inland. Now he was directing the war from there. Chungking became a capital, with temporary office buildings, resident diplomatic representatives from other countries, and even a club for them, as well as all the machinery connected with a great centre of government. Diplomats flew in and out of the strange city, which was perched on bluffs high above the river. It was still old-fashioned in many ways, yet it was now the place where strategy for something much greater than a war between only China and Japan was being developed.

CHAPTER THIRTEEN

The United States Comes to the Aid of China: The War of the South Pacific, 1941-5

Chungking, the capital of Free China, was now cut off completely from the outside world except for air transportation. Her only land contact with the sea was through the French-operated Indochina Railroad, which connected Hanoi with Kunming, capital of Yunnan Province. Even the railroad had to pass through areas that were not in China's control. Japan induced the British to close temporarily the Burma Road, which led out to Rangoon on the Bay of Bengal, sealing off Free China even more.

Now at this stage in events Japan consolidated her position in China, and no more large scale fighting took place for several years. She already controlled 170,000,000 people on thousands of square miles of the mainland. From her strong position Japan proposed the idea of forming a Greater East Asia Co-Prosperity Sphere. Asians were to cooperate with each other for the sake of their own progress and military security. Another way of putting it was, "Asia for the Asiatics." General Chiang rejected the plan publicly in December, 1938, saying that China understood Japan's friendly proposal as really meaning the destruction of an independent China and the making of her into an enslaved satellite.

"Asia for the Asiatics"

China defiant

For the next few years Free China showed great spirit, courage, and patriotism. When Japan sent her bombers over the beleaguered capital in wave after wave, the people took to the natural caves that served as air raid shelters in good humour, as though it were a normal part of everyday life. Communists and Nationalists worked together closely to resist Japan and to try to hold and rebuild what they still had. Russia stood by loyally, sending in war materials and aid by long and difficult overland routes. The watching world respected the Chinese for their endurance and honoured their government. Some called this time China's finest hour.

General Chiang had made up his mind on one thing. He would never, under any circumstances, surrender to the Japanese. He had made this decision partly because he was stubbornly courageous and partly because he counted on other countries joining China in resisting Japan. Western nations had too many interests in the Orient to let Japan dominate there, and he was sure that Japan had plans that went far beyond the conquest of China. He believed that Japan was going to confront Russia in the Far East and that she was going to challenge American naval power in the South Pacific. Why, then, should China take on this ambitious enemy alone, when she was as much the enemy of countries with better resources than Free China in her isolated condition?

While General Chiang was waiting for others to enter the struggle, cooperation between the Nationalists and the Communists began to fall apart, because the Communists were impatient and wanted to bring the war to an end without foreign involvement. Some of the young Nationalists who had studied abroad were impatient, too. They were anxious to start constructive programmes to improve and modernize their country. A man named James Yen was experimenting with improvements in rural communities and in mass education to increase literacy as quickly as possible, because he did not believe that true democracy was possible among people who could not read to inform themselves. Industrial cooperatives were expanding in number and variety and were producing both war materials and articles for everyday life. Public health work was desperately needed. But the Nationalists, following General Chiang's lead, waited for the rest of the world, and while they waited, the Communists supplied the initiative and inspiration and patriotism that the government in Chungking was allowing to weaken and die because of its policy.

Communists and Nationalists

During 1938 and 1939, while China was waiting, Japan tested out other possibilities for her own expansion. She found that Russia was not going to yield at all on border changes. In 1936 Japan and Germany had signed an anti-Comintern pact against Russian international expansion, but now Germany had involved herself in the Second World War in Europe, without consulting with her Asiatic ally at

Residents of Chungking, capital of Free China, await the last air raid warning signal before taking refuge in a cave shelter, entrance at right

Japan's position

all. It was clear that Japan could not count on Germany in the Far Eastern situation. She would have to go it alone.

The United States was still not ready to take any action against Japan, although she claimed that Japan was violating the Nine-Power Treaty of 1921. But by 1940 the relationship between the two countries was so strained that the United States decided to restrict war materials that she was sending to Japan. Scrap iron shipments were to be stopped, and the fuel oil that the Japanese Navy partly depended upon was cut back. Japanese assets in the United States were frozen. In the same year, after France had fallen to Hitler in the war in Europe, Japan turned southward and took over the northern part of what was then French Indochina, closing the railways that Free China had been able to use. In July, 1941, she decided to occupy the southern part of Indochina, as well as what she had already taken over in the north. The United States retaliated by stopping all oil ship-

Madame Chiang Kai-shek, wife of China's Generalissimo, inspects ruins in Chungking after a heavy bombing raid by Japanese planes

ments. Tension between the two countries mounted rapidly.

America steps in

The United States Secretary of State Cordell Hull tried to negotiate with the Japanese envoys who were in Washington. He proposed a delaying action, which meant that Japan would not advance any farther for a period of three months and that she would withdraw her forces from the southern part of Indochina and reduce her garrisons in that country. In return, the United States would free the restrictions she had imposed on her shipments to Japan and release the frozen Japanese assets.

The shortening fuse

General Chiang instantly rejected the whole plan. He sent cables to Prime Minister Winston Churchill in London and to the Chinese diplomats in Washington. When Cordell Hull heard about this from Winston Churchill, he set up more conferences in Washington. As a result of these, much harsher demands were suggested for Japan, and they were proposed to the Japanese ambassador to the United States in Washington on 26 November 1941. They would have meant that Japan would have to give up practically all she held on China's mainland, including Manchukuo. The American statement went even farther and declared that Japan should commit herself to support no other Chinese government but the Nationalist. Now Japan felt that there was nothing she could negotiate. The demands were too sweeping even to be discussed.

In the same year, President Franklin D. Roosevelt had included China in the Lend-Lease Act, an act of Congress which allowed the United States to give aid to countries at war with Germany. The American tide seemed to be turning more and more against Japan, but Japan had already decided on her policy. In September she looked the situation over once more to reassure herself. The proposals she received from Washington in November made her decisions seem more right than ever. She had already moved against one of her enemies, Russia, without success. Now that the United States had declared herself on the side of China, there was no time to lose. On 7 December Japanese planes bombed the American installations in Pearl Harbour and American, British, and Dutch positions in the Pacific area. The next day China formally declared war on Japan.

Pearl Harbour

The moment that General Chiang had been expecting had come. He was certain that, from now on, he would not be fighting Japan alone. The United States had certainly been helping China before this, but not formally or as a government. She had made loans before the attack on Pearl Harbour; Colonel Claire L. Chennault's Flying Tigers were already serving as an air force for China, coming in from Burma and India. But now the relationship between China and the United States was different from what it had been. From now on, the United States would be General Chiang's strong and rich ally, for her government was making a political commitment in a war that had no end in sight. China had a promise of help that seemed to assure her victory over Japan. The United States had already said that she would give up her special privileges in China, once that country was at peace, and now she repeated the promise.

Washington had a three-part objective for China. It was to help China become one of the world's great powers, to develop her military force into a modern army supported by air power, and to unify the Nationalists and Communists, once and for all.

General Chiang soon started to outline the kinds and amount of help he was going to need to wage the war. He asked the United States and Britain each for a loan of $500,000,000, as well as for huge amounts of military supplies. The United States sent Lieutenant General Joseph W. Stilwell, an experienced military man, to China to advise the Nationalist military forces. He became General Chiang's chief of staff, at the same level as the corresponding Chinese one. The United States also promoted the idea of a China-India-Burma theatre of war, partly with the idea of keeping China actively involved in fighting Japan. General Chiang was to be commander in chief of the China theatre, while General Stilwell was to be the United States commander in the China-India-Burma theatre.

Aid to China

This was an arrangement that soon caused trouble. It resulted in disagreement over how the war was to be conducted, and as time went on, this disagreement grew into near disaster. One problem was caused by the fact that all American help automatically went to the Nationalist end of the war effort, in spite of the fact that the two Chinese groups were supposed to have joined against the enemy. When no American help reached the Communist military leaders or troops, bad feeling became very strong. The war material that was poured into China stimulated hoarding and graft on the part of those in power, so that not even the Nationalist men in the field got what was intended for them. They were often ill-fed and wretchedly clothed, while it was reported that Nationalist officers and their friends were growing rich.

Quarrels

Another problem that resulted from the help that the United States was giving China was connected with General Chiang's continued unwillingness to send his forces out against Japan. Now that foreign help was arriving in such large quantity, he did not commit his men to the battle if he could avoid it.

Even though Chungking was officially sealed off from ports that were held by the Japanese, it carried on an active secret trade with Shanghai and some other ports, because it needed money. It even sold raw materials that were needed for the war for luxury items that the officials and rich people now living in the interior still craved. During 1942 and 1943 the situation was curious, because this kind of thing could go on while Free China was also demanding high patriotism from her people. The Nationalist Government wanted to strengthen its position, too, by taking advantage of events that made Russia give up areas that she had been controlling in Sinkiang Province. The Nationalist Government also tried to invade Tibet, hoping to force its local government to side with the Chungking régime, but it failed in this. Deals were constantly being made or tried, all the time behind an outward façade of unity between Communists and Nationalists.

In spite of all these developments, General Chiang kept on asking the United States for more and more help in the war, and General Stilwell was trying desperately, but without success, to get the Nationalists to throw their weight in against Japan. He failed to get the Burma campaign started at all; he could not make the Nationalists show any spirit in the battlefield.

PART THREE

Two Chinas
1943–66

Admiral Lord Louis Mountbatten and General Joseph Stilwell confer at the Burma front in March 1944

CHAPTER FOURTEEN

Nationalists Face Communists

China was proclaimed one of the Big Four powers in the Moscow Declaration of October, 1943. General Chiang, President Roosevelt, and Prime Minister Winston Churchill met in Cairo for a summit conference that December. At last, China was beginning to get the respect and consideration due her. General Chiang was promised that, at the close of the war in the Pacific, Manchuria, Formosa, and the Pescadores Islands would be returned to China and that the Allies would take action in Burma to help in the war effort. He left Cairo feeling highly encouraged.

The Moscow Declaration

After General Chiang had left, President Roosevelt, Prime Minister Churchill, and Marshal Joseph Stalin met in Tehran, Iran, for further talks. Here, plans were changed, because Russia announced that she would enter the war against Japan once the European war was over, and it seemed as if that would be soon. The Normandy landing was about to take place, and this was so much more significant to these leaders than anything connected with the Far East that the plan for Allied action in Burma was dropped.

General Chiang was extremely angry when he discovered that the strategy had been changed, and he demanded something to assure his people that the United States was still concerned about the plight of their country. What he asked for was a loan of $1,000,000,000, double the number of planes that were already planned for, and an increase in airlifted supplies so that by February, 1944, at least 20,000 tons of these would be arriving every month. The United States refused General Chiang's demands for the huge loan, and President Roosevelt was in a mood to resist other requests for help, because they were unreasonable and seemingly endless. Stalin's action against China at Tehran caused bad feeling and anxiety in China, so that the situation had worsened in more than one way.

Chiang's demands

The widening breach Things were not going well between the Nationalists and the Communists, either. General Chiang insisted that differences between the two Chinese groups were political, rather than military, and that in time they would be solved politically. The truth was that both groups were building up their military forces in order to be ready to face each other, the Communists in the northwest perfecting their guerrilla methods, which ordinary armies were not trained to handle. The division in the China front stood in the way of any real concentration on ending the war.

Colonel Claire Chennault of the Flying Tigers declared that Japan could be defeated by air power alone, using American planes based in China. The Nationalist leaders agreed with him, but General Stilwell was convinced that such attacks would fail unless China's ground forces were strong enough to defend her air bases when Japan struck back. Japan soon proved that General Stilwell's view was correct. In April, 1944, she launched sixteen divisions in a great drive through the central and eastern parts of China. Although the Nationalist forces who met them had three or four times as many men, they were defeated. The United States had paid for the airfields that were under attack, but now one after another was captured by Japan.

The United States had supported the Nationalists in good faith. She had tried to bring the two factions together. She had sent General Stilwell to help in the military organization and the training of the Chinese Army, only to have him rejected by the Nationalist leaders. The United States was beginning to lose faith in Free China. President Roosevelt had agreed to include China in the Lend-Lease Act put into effect for European countries in 1941, but he now threatened to exclude China unless General Chiang threw his weight fully into the war against Japan.

Crisis with America Events reached a state of crisis between the United States and Free China by the end of 1944, when the United States wanted to put General Stilwell in full command of the Chinese forces, because it seemed there was no other way to make China resist Japan. General Chiang was violently opposed to this plan and manœuvred things so that the general who had been familiarly and affectionately known as Vinegar Joe was called home.

A refugee train, filled and covered with civilians, leaves the war theatre in eastern China, 1944

Still, the United States Government had to keep on trying to avoid disaster in China. It sent others to advise. Vice President Henry A. Wallace, then Ambassador Patrick J. Hurley went to urge unification. General Albert C. Wedemeyer took 1,000 Americans as instructors to work at training and equipping thirty-nine Chinese divisions. In spite of these heroic efforts, it was perfectly clear that the two Chinas had such different views and aims that they could not work together.

President Roosevelt tried once more to help the Nationalist Government, by getting Russian support for it at a conference held in Yalta in February, 1945. Marshal Stalin and Prime Minister Churchill were there with President Roosevelt, discussing what the settlement terms following Japan's defeat ought to be. President Roosevelt proposed that Russian claims in northwest China be supported in exchange for Marshal Stalin's support of the Nationalist

Yalta

Refugee children on a junk going down the Yangtze River to a liberated city after he defeat of Japan

Officials review the first convoy to pass over the Ledo-Burma road as it enters China from Burma in 1945

Government. This was agreed upon, but events that followed turned things in another direction.

Japan admitted herself defeated and surrendered on 14 August 1945, following the United States' dropping of atomic bombs on Nagasaki and Hiroshima. As soon as the surrender was formally accepted, the Americans began to airlift thousands of Nationalist men into the eastern coastal areas as the Japanese pulled out, because the Communists were trying to occupy the vacuum before the Nationalists could get there. It was a race that showed the true state of affairs. It now seemed that the United States' attempt to unify the Chinese was a total failure. But the war in the Pacific was over, and the Chinese capital moved from Chungking back to Nanking and started to set its affairs in order. *Japan surrenders*

Manchuria was the main foreign problem to be faced. It continued and dramatized the competition between the two Chinese groups. Russian forces that were occupying it at the time the war ended were to withdraw within ninety days, leaving control in Nationalist hands. Nationalist military leaders gathered at the Manchurian capital, Changchun, while their forces in the northeast organized themselves, preparing to be airlifted in for the advance into Manchuria. Meanwhile, others waited in the Yangtze Valley. *Manchuria*

But the Communists also had their eyes on Manchuria, and while the Nationalists were taken in by airlift, thousands of Communist troops approached from the western province of Yunnan, where they had been in training, into the province of Shantung, where they seized control of the railways. This meant that General Chiang's men in the Yangtze Valley had no transportation to use to join their forces in the north. The Nationalists wanted the Russians to leave as agreed, but that would mean that the Communists would take over more of Manchuria, since they were on the spot, while the Nationalists were frustrated in getting there. The date when the Russians were to leave was postponed. The American General Wedemeyer, who was now advising General Chiang, urged him to move slowly, consolidating areas which he already held and connecting them by communication lines.

Such a plan did not please General Chiang, and he did

not follow it. He had six armies along the Great Wall, on the southern border of Manchuria, and he threw them against the Communists. For a time they swept the poorly equipped Reds before them, moving northward along the coast. The Nationalists took some ports along the shore of the Gulf of Chihli and then followed the corridor west of the Liaotung Peninsula toward the Manchurian capital.

General Patrick Hurley, another of the Americans sent to help China, at last came to the conclusion that his own government was acting unwisely in its policy toward China. He was entirely disillusioned about the Chinese, and he resigned as his country's ambassador in November, 1945. But the United States still did not give up. In December she sent General George C. Marshall to try once more to mediate between the Chinese. His gentlemanly bearing and quiet personality appealed to the Chinese officials. For a few months it seemed barely possible that he might succeed in his proposals for a coalition government. A cease-fire order

General Marshall

Generalissimo Chiang Kai-shek signs the document that indicates China's ratification of the United Nations Charter, 1945

General George C. Marshall who made every attempt to unify the Nationalist and Communist forces of China against Japan

was sent out over the country, and the resulting truce was monitored by teams made up of paired Americans and Chinese, who were located in even the most out-of-the-way places, to see that the fighting was actually stopped. Perhaps even General Marshall was surprised at his success.

But Nationalist China had not allowed the truce plan to be used in Manchuria, and this threatened what General Marshall was trying to accomplish. Manchuria was the main factor in the civil war that began now. The Russians delayed turning over their holdings in Manchuria even longer because of the sudden strength of the Communists. Russian troops had disarmed the Japanese Manchukuo Army of more than 300,000 men when the war ended, and when the Chinese Communists arrived, they had recruited these men into their ranks. They had also taken over the stockpiles of arms and munitions that the Japanese left behind. This meant that the Chinese Communists had been able to get a large number of trained men and a good supply of war materials. Russia had to wait until the Nationalists could

Civil war

strengthen their position in the area, and this took time.

Finally, in March, 1946, Russia started to withdraw from Manchuria. A few days later General Chiang's men replaced the Russians in Mukden, and at the same time General Marshall left for Washington for consultation. When he returned a month later, he found that things had grown worse. The truce system, which General Chiang had by now accepted for Manchuria, had broken down. The Communists were taking over the areas vacated by the Russians, so that they now controlled all of northern Manchuria and much of northeast China.

Talks between General Marshall, Chou En-lai, representing the Communists, and General Chiang could not get anywhere, because General Chiang was not willing to go halfway. Instead, he acted by moving his forces northward. This resulted in the Communists coming in from the south and taking over important industrial centres. A whole Nationalist army went over to the Communists. Although the fighting swung back and forth, the Communist threat was growing steadily stronger.

Peace proposals At this point, General Chiang returned to Nanking and said that he was willing to discuss the situation with General Marshall again. A fifteen-day truce was agreed upon, and during this time, General Chiang presented some proposals for peace, but they were not acceptable to the Communists. The truce was extended while peace proposals were worked over again. General Marshall went back and forth between the two parties, trying desperately to find some way of halting the civil war. After the truce was over, each side expressed appreciation for General Marshall's patient efforts and declared its love of peace. But the truth was that General Marshall had failed. There now seemed to be no way of avoiding full-scale war between the two Chinese political groups.

The Nationalists certainly appeared to be much better prepared than the less well-organized Communists. Because of the enormous help which the United States had provided, Nationalist China was much richer after the war in the Pacific than she had been before. Most of the fighting had been aimed at Japanese targets or targets at sea, so that the Chinese countryside did not show great war destruction.

United Nations Relief and Rehabilitation Administration flour being unloaded from an American ship off Shanghai's famous Bund, after the war in the Pacific ended

The Japanese had also enriched China by leaving industries behind, and these supplied coal, iron, and electricity that had not been available before. In spite of this increase in wealth, an organization known as **UNRRA** (United Nations Relief and Rehabilitation Administration) came in to help after the war was over and supplied China with more than $600,000,000's worth of assistance, two-thirds in money and the rest in goods.

UNRRA

Although all attempts at truce and negotiation had been given up by the summer of 1946, and Nationalist Armies were already active in the north, Chou En-lai and General Marshall were still in Nanking. The American ambassador Dr J. Leighton Stuart, arrived and met with General Chiang and the Communist leader in the hope of even now being able to avoid a greater war. But in August the United States Government sold the Nationalist Government war supplies valued at $900,000,000 at bargain prices, and this did not help the negotiations. While these goods had been intended for American armed forces, they were now labelled for civilian use. Chou En-lai was quick to see that the motor-cycles, trucks, communications equipment, and medical supplies would be immensely useful in warfare.

American involvement

Nothing could stop the steady drift toward open civil war now. Yet, even though it was a civil war, the United States could not disentangle herself from it because of the support she had long ago started to provide to what at that time had seemed to be the authentic China, which was struggling to modernize herself along democratic lines. The United States tried to take some steps to disengage herself by withdrawing her advisers and ending her official efforts to negotiate. She also withdrew her Marines from North China and reduced the American forces stationed in China to one-tenth of what they had been.

Nationalist weaknesses

The Nationalists were weakened for two reasons. The first was that their armies were poorly led, often by officers who were so dishonest that they were thinking only of what they could get for themselves, rather than of the condition of their country. Strategy was not well-planned by such leaders; nor was it even carried out by the troops if they did not like it. The second weakening factor was inflation. It had begun before Japan's defeat, because Free China was then spending far more than her income. Prices doubled every few weeks as the value of money decreased. A currency reform plan was attempted, but it failed in a few months. Middle-class Chinese, who had wanted to support the Nationalist programme for the country, lost all faith in their government when the new currency plan collapsed.

Each year that passed brought more defeats to General Chiang's armies in the field. Action first centred in Manchuria, where the Communists held the communication lines so that they could isolate the Nationalists from one another. General Chiang tried to get his men out of Manchuria, directing the operation himself from Peiping. The Communists attacked the port of Hulutao on the Gulf of Chihli, where he had 11 of his divisions. Some of the divisions went right over to the enemy side, and the rest found themselves so poorly supported that they escaped. Another 8 divisions located in an important town not far away surrendered to the Communists at once, without resisting. Still others did the same thing and even joined in the battle against the Nationalists. None of the Nationalist forces seemed ready to stand firm in this engagement. On 5 November 1948, General Chiang withdrew from Hulutao, which he had set his heart on keeping as a beachhead, and knew that he had lost Manchuria. During 1947 and 1948 he also lost 400,000 of his men and large quantities of the supplies provided by the United States.

Now action concentrated in Central China. Beginning early in November, one of the greatest single battles of modern times took place. It was that of Huai-hai, in the Huai River basin almost 100 miles north of Nanking, of which the city of Hsuchow is the key point. General Chiang threw in 50 of the 200 divisions he still had left and directed the action from Nanking. The Communists were at an advantage, because they controlled the villages in the area, and the villagers were on their side. They set the railroads that had been idle running, moving their men and supplies. In two weeks the Communists had cut off or encircled 300,000 of the Nationalist men. General Chiang sent in a relief of 120,000 American-trained troops. It was useless. By the end of January, 1949, he knew that he was defeated. He had lost the last of the 39 divisions that America had trained and equipped; the Communists had captured huge amounts of war materials. Worst of all, the way to Nanking now lay open. The enemy had only to move in.

Huai-hai

The Nationalists were totally defeated. Tientsin and Peiping surrendered in January, 1949. The Communists crossed the Yangtze River the next spring and took Nanking while the Nationalist Government fled first to Canton and then to its old post in Chungking. At the same time, province after province went into Communist hands. By October most of China was theirs. They formally installed themselves as the Central People's Government of the People's Republic of China in Peiping, which they renamed the Northern Capital, or Peking, once more.

Nationalists crushed

In the south General Chiang moved the Nationalist capital from Chungking, farther up the river to Chengtu, Szechuan. Everyone knew that each move was no more than a delaying action. Nationalist China, which had for so long drawn the sympathy and loyalty of world democracy as Free China, was being pushed from the mainland after twenty-one years of struggle.

A complex failure

What had happened was not only a story of war and defeat, of division and civil war. It was a story of personality struggles among the Chinese leaders; of stubbornness on the part of General Chiang; and most of all, of his failure to understand what Dr Sun Yat-sen had hoped to accomplish by the revolution, what democracy really was, and what personal devotion to a cause might cost. He had failed to bring better times to his own poor and oppressed; he had not freed them from war or invasion or inflation or illiteracy. When he had at last to escape from Chengtu, the Communists swarming in as his plane rose dramatically above the city, he had Formosa all prepared as a place of exile for his government. Taipeh on the island of Formosa became the capital of General Chiang Kai-shek's government-in-exile.

CHAPTER FIFTEEN

Mainland China

The Communists in Peking enthusiastically proclaimed themselves masters of the mainland on 1 October 1949. Although all of the mainland and the island of Hainan, historically Chinese, were not occupied by the Communists until May, 1950, the People's Republic of China began to celebrate October 1 as a festival on this day of its inauguration and have continued to do so. Mao Tse-tung, most often referred to as Chairman Mao, chairman of the Central Committee of the Chinese Communist Party, gave a great speech praising the success of the party. Foreign countries were invited to recognize the new government. Russia did so at once and sent her ambassador to Peking within a few days. *The People's Republic*

In December, 1949, Chairman Mao went to Moscow to discuss how much political, military, and economic aid China could expect from Russia. A treaty that assured Mao of a good proportion of what he had hoped for was drawn up.

Great changes soon took place in the Communist party. The 1,210,000 members of 1945 had by now increased to five times that number. It purged its membership now, restated its principles, and tightened its policies in order to be ready to carry forward its great plans. China's new leaders were starting a tremendous programme that was to change the life of the country. In October, 1951, they initiated the five Anti-campaigns against the merchant class. The five things to be ended by these were bribery, tax evasion, fraud, stealing of state property, and stealing of state secrets. *Communist policy*

The new government attacked the landlord system. Landlords often owned fields that added up to 40 or so acres, a large area for China, which they rented out in small plots to tenant farmers, who lived on them and worked them, paying outrageously high rentals. The landlords lived comfortably and idly in town on what they collected. Farmers often fell behind in their payments and had to borrow. These debts could be held against them by loan agents or even the landlords themselves, at such high rates of interest that they kept mounting and could never be paid off.

When the Communists went into Manchuria in 1948, they had started a programme of land reform there. The government was to take over all farmland and redivide it among the farmers. The government was also to take control of farm tools, farm animals, stores of grain, and the houses of the landlords, who were to get their share in the redistribution, like everyone else, unless they were "enemies of the people". Even among the peasants, the richer ones were to be levelled down, while the poorer were to be raised to a higher standard of living. Often, private holdings, such as monasteries, temples, and mission properties, including churches, were confiscated and added to the pool of land and properties that were to be redivided.

In 1950, two years after this system was tried out in Manchuria, it was announced for the whole country. It was put into motion by small teams, or cadres, of people, who went into the villages; set up courts, or tribunals; held trials, or accusation meetings, and announced their judgments of guilt on landlords and gentry. Decisions that were made in this way were served on the culprits thoroughly and without mercy. No one was spared in the bloody purge. Several million people were reported to have lost their lives. One important result of the terrible affair and the method used to bring it about was that for the first time peasants found themselves taking part in the action of their government and responsible to it. Another result, of course, was that the land was actually redivided. Each farm family, estimated at five members, now had about $2\frac{1}{2}$ acres of good land. Mutual aid teams, organized by the government, helped wherever they were needed in busy seasons. This plan gradually led to the forming of large collective farms, or joint-ownership farms. Later it was to develop into a commune system.

Foreigners   The Peking government made a clean sweep of foreign enterprises and missionary projects. It seized foreign investments and tried to clear the country of imperialism. The British lost an estimated $800,000,000, the Americans much less, because their investments were smaller. At the same time, all the help that they had poured into supporting the

Nationalist Government was also their loss. The Japanese were the greatest losers of all, as far as industries were concerned. These were still less important to her than the fact that she had failed to add what she had hoped for of the mainland to her empire. With foreign investments liquidated and treaty ports closed, Communist China looked inward. Shanghai, which had been the greatest trading centre of the Far East, began to die.

The new China had relations only with Russia at this point. Russia gave up her rights to railroads in Manchuria and to the ports on the northern shores where she had held privileges. China and Russia established joint companies to organize an airline between the two countries and to develop petroleum and other mineral products in Sinkiang Province, China's most northwesterly area. Russia also furnished China with technicians. The fact that China could trade with Russia was the most important advantage of all, because other foreign trade channels were now closed. *Russia*

Communist China soon turned her attention to Korea, because she considered that country a necessary part of her national defence system. Hostility toward the United States in connection with Korea had begun in 1947. At the time of the Japanese surrender, Korea had been divided at the Thirty-eighth parallel, Russian troops coming into North Korea above it and American troops into South Korea. A Communist government took shape in the north, while in the south the United States supported a military government until the formation of the Republic of Korea in 1948. At that time American forces were withdrawn except for a token advisory group. Russia also announced the withdrawal of her troops from North Korea, but the Communist Democratic People's Republic of Korea was strong there, and the Thirty-eighth parallel became a battle line between north and south. Raids from the north were reported first, and then, in June, 1950, the Communist North Korean Army struck across the line. *The Korean War*

The United States at once took two actions. She intervened in the Korean situation in the name of the United Nations, and she stationed the United States' seventh fleet in the Formosa Strait. The Nationalist Government on the island was jubilant. The United States was still its protector.

On the mainland, on the other hand, when the North Korean forces were thrown back almost as far as the Yalu River, Chinese Communist forces poured in to help North Korea. Mao Tse-tung already considered the United States China's enemy; now he considered her an invader. Although American troops had been withdrawn from South Korea in 1949, the Communists in Peking now complained that the United States was setting up a defence line in the Pacific, with strong influence over the government of South Korea and with occupation forces in Japan. It was true that the United States and the Seoul government had signed a mutual defence assistance plan in June, 1950. The Peking government pointed to it as evidence of their complaint and arrayed its People's Liberation Army in a line along the coastal areas facing on Formosa.

The Korean War went on for three years, with bitter losses among the Koreans, North and South, the Chinese, and the Americans who soon were playing a major role on behalf of South Korea. After the Korean truce was signed in October, 1953, China began to build up her economy as quickly as possible. One of Dr Sun Yat-sen's purposes had been to raise the standard of living for everyone. Even with land reform, it was still at poverty level for millions. Iron ore, coal, industrial minerals, and oil lay under China's fields and mountains. They had to be developed. In the years 1950, 1951, and 1952 crops had been good. In 1953 the government proclaimed a great five-year plan, although it had very little to base such a plan on. China had closed her doors to the possibility of getting loans for investment from the outside, because she had stopped foreign trade. She could not get Communist help except from Russia. She needed not only money but skilled technicians to carry on the work that had been done by foreigners before.

Peking argued that it must be possible to get money in some way. Mao Tse-tung had obtained a loan of $300,000,000 from Moscow, to be repaid in amounts of $60,000,000 a year for five years, but that was almost used up by the end of 1952. A meeting called by a Communist-led group, the World Peace Council, met that year in Moscow. This seemed to be a chance to get help. At this time Peking did succeed in getting trade agreements signed with private

Prime Minister Chou En-lai at an exhibition of children's building models in Peking

businessmen from eleven non-Communist countries. These included Britain, France, West Germany, Belgium, the Netherlands, Switzerland, and Italy. Although some of these agreements could not be implemented because of national restrictions, they were the first sign that Peking wanted to have trade relations with Europe.

At the end of the same year Chou En-lai, who was now premier of the Peking government, led a delegation to Moscow to get more aid. Russia at last agreed to help China build more than 100 industrial plants. These were to be paid for in China's raw materials. Russia also gave China a loan of $430,000,000 on credit to help carry out the first five-year plan. In 1954 joint projects for producing oil and mineral products and the air transportation system were put entirely into Chinese hands. During the first ten years of the Chinese Communist régime, Russia would also meet the costs of sending 6,500 Chinese students to Moscow to study, on a

Help from Russia

The five-year plans

loan basis that was to be repaid over a long period of time.

Peking now planned three five-year plans, extending from 1952 to 1967. By the year 2000 China was to be a world power, economically, as well as in every other way. The Communist Government was measuring her plans against Russia's progress, but it had far less to invest, a much poorer communications system, and the unexpected and costly Korean War. It also failed to allow for its population growth. Enormous pressure was put on the farmers and the industrial workers to produce. Propaganda teams toured the countryside, singing and dramatizing the goals of the new government to whip up patriotism and enthusiasm. They presented the people with the vision of a new day, and for a time the people gave all they had to make it come true.

CHAPTER SIXTEEN

At the Crossroads

The war in Korea increased the misunderstanding between Communist China and the United States. Misunderstanding was increased, too, because the United States supported the French colonial war in Indochina, which was going on between 1946 and 1954, while China sided with the revolutionists there. American support for the Nationalists in Formosa and the seventh fleet lying in the strait did not improve relations.

In September, 1954, the United States, Britain, France, Australia, and New Zealand joined the Philippines, Thailand, and Pakistan to form SEATO or the Southeast Asia Treaty Organization. This pact would link the major non-Communist nations bordering on mainland China to help maintain their security. India, Burma, and Indonesia had officially recognized the government in Peking, so they could not be included. The government of South Korea, strongly supported by the United States, was afraid of Japan and would not have her in the pact. While SEATO might help in holding the line against Communism, countries within Asia were groping to find some way of checking what they believed was their gradual encirclement by Western military power. They called a conference in Bandung, Indonesia. Twenty-nine Asian and African countries assembled there in April, 1955. Chou En-lai was the spokesman for Peking. North and South Korea, as well as Formosa, were not represented, but the Philippines, Thailand, and Pakistan, which were also SEATO members, were there. Prime Minister Nehru of India declared for the group that the countries which met in Bandung were not opposing anyone, but they did not want to take part in quarrels or conquests of the Western nations, either. They wanted to be let alone to develop their own freedom and nationalism.

In Moscow Nikita Khrushchev, who was soon to become

SEATO

Soviet premier, denounced Stalin and his opinions, giving a new and more imaginative direction to Russia's Communism. This affected Russia's relationship with China's leaders in Peking, because they had been devoted to Joseph Stalin's theories. But in 1957 Peking, too, did some experimenting with freer thinking among her intellectuals, calling it the Spring of One Hundred Flowers. This new freedom allowed criticism even of the government, as the earlier policy certainly had not. A bitter and scathing appraisal of the Communist system resulted.

The Spring of One Hundred Flowers

The experiment in freer expression in China, which grew out of the change in Russia, came to an abrupt end when the Peking government reversed its policy after six weeks. It was now more severe than ever in repressing any except approved statements. The first five-year plan also came to an end in 1957. The government had succeeded in reaching some of its industrial objectives, but agricultural production had fallen far behind the goals set, although agricultural production was crucial.

Chairman Mao attended a meeting in Moscow, which celebrated the fortieth anniversary of the Russian Revolution, in late 1957. He hoped to get Russia to join his country in opposition to Western imperialism, to stop giving aid to other countries in order to concentrate it more on China, and to get Russia to forgive some of the debts Peking had incurred, but he failed in these objectives. What could be done? China was now in desperate straits. She had planned to begin another five-year plan in 1958. To delay or to give it up would be an admission of her inability to take her place in the world. She proudly decided to launch a three-year intensive programme called the Great Leap Forward.

The Great Leap Forward

A call went out over the country, and popular support for the new idea was whipped up by high-powered propaganda. Small, primitive furnaces were built in backyards in towns and cities or behind farmhouses to make steel from scrap iron gathered wherever it could be found. Dikes were rebuilt, canals dredged; large dams begun to carry out irrigation projects. A few years before this, China had talked of an eight-hour day for everyone, but now the workday sometimes stretched to twice that. Babies and small children were taken care of in nurseries and day care centres so that

Derrick connected with blast furnace in iron works near Peking—a sign of modernization of industry under Communist Government

women would be able to work like men. The spirit of achievement, of hope, of national pride caught up the people because of expert propaganda and probably because they were afraid not to fall in line.

Communes   Peking decided to take an even more drastic step to increase farm output during the first year of the Great Leap Forward. Farm cooperatives, which had been in operation for several years, were now combined into still larger units called communes in order to be better managed and controlled. Industry, trade, education, and social and military life all were affected by the idea. Families were separated, so that men were in one place, women in another, and children in still another. Groups ate in mess halls, instead of cooking for themselves. Nothing was personal or private. Everything was pooled and then rationed out. Those from outside who were able to observe the Chinese during this period reported that they seemed to be in a kind of frenzy to succeed, devoted to a plan to which they were totally committed. There was even a report that Communist China was going to overtake Soviet Russia in reaching total Communism.

Peking officially announced enormous progress at the end of 1958. Farm production, as well as that of iron and steel, was said to have been doubled. Production of machine tools was reportedly three times what it had been. Oil production and electric power were well up. Claims that new sources of minerals had been found sounded encouraging. But the report was so fantastically good that many people did not believe it.

An exhausted people   This kind of pressure to produce could not be kept up for long. People gradually became exhausted. After long hours of work, they still had to go through hours of propaganda lectures and study. Homes had been broken up in the commune system, and this caused secret resentment. Tools that now belonged to the government were not taken care of as well as when they belonged to a man and his family. Much of the great effort began to seem futile.

At last the government decided to modify the commune system so that each commune was self-supporting. Families were joined together again, could have gardens for their own use, and could take on small side jobs to earn a little money for themselves. The workday was shortened. In many cases, the communes became not much more than groups of family villages organized to produce as much as possible under heavy propaganda.

Propaganda

During 1958, 1959, and 1960 production levels were lower, although the figures that were given out were always encouraging. Propaganda poured out of Peking in a continuous stream, carried by loudspeakers all over the country. One drive followed another, urging efficiency and speed. Sometimes foolish things were done, as when a drive to wipe out sparrows because they ate grain was begun and resulted in the discovery that the insects that the sparrows had been eating were far more destructive than the birds themselves. In spite of the great pressure, speed, and urgency of the Great Leap Forward, it failed.

While Peking was concentrating on its economy, it was not paying much attention to its relations with foreign countries. Although fourteen non-Communist countries recognized the Communist Government during 1949 and 1950, it had set up formal relations with only six of them. These were

A scene from the classic opera revived by the Communist government. This presentation of *The Wild Goose* won first prize at the Warsaw Festival

Communist China today is an atomic power. Here, her famous nuclear physicist, Tsien San-tsiang, signs autographs for admirers

Burma, India, Indonesia, Switzerland, Sweden, and Denmark. It delayed formal diplomatic relations with the other eight, Britain, Pakistan, Ceylon, Afghanistan, Norway, Finland, the Netherlands, and Israel. After her consul in Mukden was mistreated and then arrested in 1949, the United States recalled all of her officials. The United States consulate in Peking was seized in 1950.

China's trade status

Perhaps Communist China's real relationship with both Communist and non-Communist countries was shown most clearly by her trade status. After the truce in Korea, China wanted freer trade, and by 1957 most of the important trading countries, with the exception of the United States, were doing business with Communist China, just as they were with other Communist countries. Peking's foreign trade began to climb steadily, so that it neared the level that it had reached before the Communists took over the country.

Peking began to give assistance to other countries by 1953, although it was still trying to establish its own economy. China could give her political views along with her aid, and this interested her. She first helped North Korea, then North Vietnam and Outer Mongolia. In 1956 she began to assist non-Communist countries, beginning with Cambodia, Nepal, Egypt, Ceylon, and then Indonesia. By 1961 she was sending out as much foreign aid in proportion to her national income as the United States was.

The Chinese Communists were succeeding in many things, in spite of great failures in others. They had changed their whole pattern of living and their whole system of economy. Public sanitation had been started, flies and mosquitoes had almost disappeared; epidemics were under control; irrigation had been immensely improved; roads, railways, and air service were better than ever in China's history. The public was informed, because loudspeakers kept up a continuous stream of Peking-controlled news. Literacy had increased dramatically through enforced study classes. While China was still a poor country, the lives of even the poorest were better than they had ever been.

Communist achievements

All of these things had grown out of a dream – first that of Sun Yat-sen and then that of Mao Tse-tung. In 1966 Mao Tse-tung was still dreaming, although he was seventy-three years old. But the time had come when his huge country could not go any farther on propaganda and dreams. It had to compete in a modern world if it was still to be the Middle Kingdom in such a world. Men who were younger than Mao saw that China was going to have to change her methods and be guided by people with expert abilities, rather than by visionaries, if she was to go forward. Her leadership fell into two groups – those who clung to the old, visionary propaganda of the Mao of the Long March and those who thought about taking practical steps.

The outside world knew that some great churning was going on in Red China, but it could not find out exactly what it was about, because so few foreigners were allowed to enter the country. The reports of those who did get in did not always agree, because they looked at things from different angles, depending upon their own national backgrounds.

As more disruption developed in China, bands of young people roved across the country and through the towns, shouting and singing slogans. Their words came from little red books bearing the title *Quotations from Chairman Mao Tse-tung*. The little red book, translated into many languages, became an international best seller. The young people who were responding to the thrilling history of Chairman Mao were the Red Guards. While old friends supported Chairman

Mao's best seller

"While the students' main task is to study, they should in addition to their studies learn other things, that is, industrial work, farming and military affairs. They should also criticize the bourgeoisie. The period of schooling should be shortened, education should be revolutionized, and the domination of our schools by bourgeois intellectuals should by no means be allowed to continue." A quotation from Chairman Mao Tse-tung

A new Middle Kingdom

Mao, younger men waited, because they knew that the Red Guards had come too late.

China had been in turmoil for 100 years, looking for a new form of government, a new and better life for her millions, recognition that she was still the Middle Kingdom in a modern world. The germ of change had come from the West had sprouted, almost died, then twisted into a new and strange shape as it grew to enormous size. Communist leaders had taken over the original ideas of democratic revolution begun by Sun Yat-sen. They were dominated by the personality of Mao Tse-tung, but when he was gone, would China become more Chinese again? Would life soften, individuals be identified, instead of being lost in the masses? No one really knew.

Formosa

The Nationalist Government on Formosa was dominated by one personality, too. General Chiang Kai-shek, who was eighty in 1966, had made the island into a demonstration of all that he had declared he could do with the mainland. He had carried out land reforms with the help of the American Joint Commission on Rural Reconstruction. Irrigation, forestry, soil conservation, health measures, crop improvement all had progressed well, heavily supported by American funds and technical know-how. Industrial output had greatly increased over what it had been.

The United States seventh fleet still lay in the strait, an important link in her Far Eastern line of defence. While this fact gave General Chiang security, it divided the Communists and non-Communists more than ever. Mainland China lay just 150 miles across the strait from Formosa, and beyond and to the north lay Russia. Communist China's claims of the United States' Far Eastern aims seemed justified.

The future

The two old men at the head of the two Chinas had both been shaped by Sun Yat-sen's dreams. When they die, perhaps younger men will find some way to join the two parts of China again. Some said that such plans were already well-laid. Everyone knew that China was still one nation and the Chinese one people, regardless of how it might appear.

Table of Main Dates

1842   Treaty of Nanking resulting from First Opium War gives Great Britain lease on Hong Kong and other valuable rights.

1895   War with Japan results in ignominious Treaty of Shimonoseki.

1898   Emperor Kuang Hsu starts the One Hundred Days of Reform in Peking.

1899   The Boxer rebellion is suppressed by foreign troops.

1911   The Chinese Nationalist Revolution led by Sun Yat-sen replaces the old Manchu rule by a republic.

1917   China enters the First World War on the side of the Allies.

1919   Treaty of Versailles disappoints all China's hopes in the war.

1921   The Chinese Communist Party is born.

1925   Sun Yat-sen fails to unify the two seats of Chinese government at Canton and Peking.

1926–7   Chiang Kai-shek assumes leadership of the Nationalist Party in Canton, and marches towards Peking. But he sets up his Nationalist capital in Nanking.

1927   Chinese Communists who are attacked by Chiang Kai-shek move to Kiangsi Province under the leadership of Mao Tse-tung.

1928   Chiang Kai-shek brings all China under the Nationalist flag.

1931   Japan seizes Manchuria in a clash with Nationalist forces.

1934   The Chinese people clamor for stronger opposition to Japan. Chiang Kai-shek concentrates on wiping out the Communists. The Communist forces escape him and begin the Long March of 6,000 miles to the northwest.

1936   Chiang Kai-shek is kidnapped in an attempt to make him unite Communists and Nationalists in the struggle against Japan.

1937   Japan invades China and occupies Nanking. The Nationalists move capital of Free China to Chungking.

1941	After Japan bombs Pearl Harbour, the United States comes to the aid of Free China.
1943	Cairo summit conference; China is promised the return of Chinese territory after the war, but the promises were later changed.
1945	Japan admits defeat after atomic bombs are dropped on Hiroshima and Nagasaki. Chiang Kai-shek accepts her surrender through his representatives at Nanking.
1949	The Nationalist forces are pushed by the Communists from mainland China to Taiwan (Formosa). The Communists proclaim the Central People's Government of the Chinese People's Republic in Peking.

Suggestions for Further Reading

BARNETT, A. DOAK, *Communist China and Asia.* New York, Vintage Books (Random House), 1961.
CLUBB, O. EDMUND, *Twentieth-Century China.* New York, Columbia University Press, 1964.
FAIRBANK, JOHN KING, *The United States and China.* Cambridge, Harvard University Press, 1946.
FITZGERALD, C. P., *The Birth of Communist China.* Baltimore, Penguin Books, 1964.
LATOURETTE, KENNETH A., *The Chinese: Their History and Culture.* New York, The Macmillan Company, 1934.
MCALEAVY, HENRY, *The Modern History of China.* New York, Frederick A. Praeger, Inc. Publishers, 1967.
SEWELL, WILLIAM G., *I Stayed in China.* London, George Allen and Unwin, Ltd., 1966.
SNOW, EDGAR, *Red Star over China.* New York, Random House, 1944. New York, Grove Press, 1961.
Encyclopaedia Britannica, Vol. 5. 1959 edition.

Index

Atomic bombs, 85

Bandung, Conference, 99
Borodin, Michael, 47, 48
Boxers (Righteous Harmony Fists), Boxer Uprising, 32, 33, 35, 43
Britain, British, 9, 13, 14, 15, 16, 17, 18, 24, 25, 26, 27, 34, 43, 48, 49
British and American Tobacco Company, 36
Burlingame, Anson, 20
Burma, 25; (China-India-Burma Theatre), 76, 77, 78, 81

Cairo, Summit Conference, 81
Canton, 17, 21, 27, 39, 40, 43, 46, 47, 49, 60, 62
Central People's Government of the People's Republic of China, 91, 93
Chang Hsueh-liang (see Young Marshal)
Chang Tso-lin, General, 48, 51
Chen Chiung-ming, 46, 47
Chengtu, Szechwan (as Nationalist capital), 91, 92
Chennault, Colonel Claire of Flying Tigers, 76, 82
Chiang Kai-shek, 47, 49, 50, 51, 52, 53, 54, 55, 58, 59, 60, 61, 62, 63, 64, 65, 72, 73, 75, 76, 81, 85, 89, 90, 91, 92, 107
Chinese Revolution, 40, 41, 42, 45, 47, 50, 52
Chino-Japanese War, First, 23, 24, 40; Second, beginning, 66
Chou En-lai, 51, 59, 88, 89, 90, 97, 99
Chungking, Szechwan (as Nationalist capital), 70, 71, 73, 77, 85, 87, 91
Churchill, Prime Minister Winston, 75, 81, 83
Comintern, 47, 75
Communes, 102, 103
Communism, Communists, 12, 45, 46, 47, 49, 50, 51, 52, 54, 55, 58, 60, 61, 63, 64, 66, 67, 68, 77, 82, 85, 86, 87, 89, 91, 92, 93, 94, 95, 98, 103, 105, 106
Cushing, Caleb, 15
Customs, duty on imports, 16, 18, 27

Donald, William Henry, 64

East India Company, 13, 27
Extraterritoriality, 15, 17, 18, 19, 21, 24, 32, 35, 53

Feng Yu-hsiang, General, 48, 54
Five Year Plans, 96, 97, 98, 100
Formosa (Taiwan), 23, 26, 92; Strait, 95, 99, 106
France, French, 9, 15, 17, 18, 24, 25, 26, 40, 43, 44
Free China, 70, 72, 73, 74, 78, 82, 90, 92

German, Germany, 24, 25, 32, 33, 43, 53, 60, 62, 67, 68, 73, 74, 76
Gordon, C. G., 16
Great Leap Forward, 100, 102, 103
Great Wall, 9, 26, 61, 86

Hankow, 42, 49, 50, 54, 70
Hart, Sir Robert, 17
Hawaii, 28, 38, 40
Hay, John, 27, 28
Hong Kong, 15, 26, 40, 48
Hsin Chung Hui (Revive China Society), 40, 41
Hull, Cordell, Secretary of State, 75
Hundred Days of Reform, 31
Hurley, Ambassador Patrick, J., 83, 86
Hu Shih, Dr., and literary Revolution, 44

Indemnity, 23, 24, 33, 35
India, 9, 13, 14, 25, 26
Indochina (Vietnam, Laos, Cambodia), 25, 72, 74, 75, 99

Japan, 9, 23, 24, 31, 34, 36, 38, 40, 41, 43, 44, 48, 54, 55, 58, 62, 64, 66, 67, 68, 69, 70, 71, 72, 75, 83, 85, 88, 89, 90, 99
Joffe, Adolf, 47

K'ang Yu-wei, 31
Khrushchev, Premier Nikita, S., 99–100
Kidnapping, of Chiang Kai-shek, 63, 64
Korea, 23, 25, 34, 95, 96, 98, 99
Kuang Hsu, Emperor, 19, 31, 32, 37
Kuomintang (see Nationalist Party)

Land Reform, 93, 94, 96
League of Nations, 58
Lend-Lease Act, 76
Li Hung-chang, Viceroy, 20, 21, 23, 38
Liang Ch'i-chao, 31
Liaotung Peninsula, 23, 26, 34, 86
Long March, 61, 63, 105
Lytton Commission, 58

Manchu, Manchus, 9, 11, 14, 19, 22, 36, 37, 38, 40, 41, 42, 45
Manchukuo, 55, 58, 66, 78, 87
Manchuria, 23, 25, 34, 51, 54, 55, 85, 86, 87, 88, 90, 91
Mao Tse-tung, 51, 60, 93, 96, 100, 105, 106
Marshall, General George C., 86, 87, 88, 89

111

May Fourth Movement, 44, 45, 69
Missions, Missionaries, 9, 16, 17, 21, 24, 32, 38, 40, 50, 94
Moscow, 47, 52, 54, 60, 81, 93, 94, 96, 97, 99, 100
Most-Favoured-Nation Clause, 27
Mukden, 55

Nanking, Nanking Government, 16, 19, 50, 51, 53, 54, 58, 61, 62, 63, 64, 66, 67, 68, 69, 70, 85
Nationalist Party (Kuomintang), Nationalist, 42, 46, 47, 48, 49, 50, 51, 52, 53, 54, 59, 62, 64, 65, 66, 72, 73, 75, 76, 77, 78, 82, 83, 85, 87, 88, 90, 92, 95, 99, 106
Nehru, Prime Minister of India, 99
New Life Movement, 59
Nine-Power Treaty, 47, 74
Northern Expedition, 46, 48, 49, 50, 51

October First Celebration, 93
Open Door Policy, 27, 28, 47
Opium, 13, 14, 19, 35; Opium War (First), 14, 16, 27; (Second), 17

Peace Conference, 43, 44
Pearl Harbour, 76
Peking (Peiping), 9, 11, 14, 15, 16, 17, 18, 20, 21, 23, 32, 35, 40, 42, 44, 46, 48, 49, 50, 51, 66, 67, 68, 69, 90, 91, 94, 96, 97, 99, 100, 102, 103
Portuguese, 9, 13

Quotations from Chairman Mao, 105

Railroads, 25, 26, 34, 36, 43, 54, 55, 95
Roosevelt, President Franklin D., 76, 81, 83
Roosevelt, President Theodore, 34
Russia, Soviet, 17, 24, 26, 34, 46, 47, 48, 50, 51, 54, 62, 63, 66, 68, 72, 76, 85, 86, 88, 95, 100, 106, 107

Secret Societies, 16, 37, 41, 52
Shanghai, 44, 45, 47, 48, 50, 52, 53, 55, 58, 68, 69, 77, 95
Shantung, Province, 23, 25, 26, 43, 44, 68, 69
Sian, 32, 35, 61, 63, 64, 65
Soong (family), 52; (Mayling), 53, 59
Southeast Asia Treaty Organization, 99
Spain, 9, 28
Spheres of Influence, 26, 27
Spring of One Hundred Flowers, 100
Stalin, Marshal Joseph, 81, 83, 100
Standard Oil Company of New York, 36
Stilwell, General Joseph W., 77, 78, 82
Sun Yat-sen, 21, 38, 39, 40, 41, 42, 43, 45, 46, 47, 48, 49 (death), 50, 51, 52, 53, 92, 96, 105, 107

Taierchwang, Battle of, 70
Taiping Rebellion, 16, 18, 19
Tehran (Summit Conference), 81
"Three Principles of the People", 41
Tientsin, 17, 18, 25, 26, 49, 68
Trade of Communist China, 104
Treaty of Nanking, 14, 15, 27

Treaty of Portsmouth, 34
Treaty of Shimonoseki, 23
Treaty of Tientsin, 17, 18, 25, 26
Treaty of Versailles, 44
Tseng Kuo-fan, 16, 19, 20
Tsungli Yamen, 17, 20
T'ung Meng Hui (Revolutionary Alliance), 41, 42
Twenty-One Demands, 43, 44
T'zu Hsi, Empress Dowager, 19, 20, 21, 31, 32, 35, 37

United Nations, 89, 95
United Nations Relief and Rehabilitation administration, 89
United States, 13, 14, 15, 16, 17, 20, 27, 28, 34, 38, 42, 47, 48, 59, 67, 74, 77, 81, 82, 86, 87, 90, 91, 94, 95, 96, 99, 107

Wallace, Vice-President Henry A., 80
Ward, Frederick Townsend, 16
Washington Conference, 47, 53
Wedemeyer, General Albert C., 83, 85
Western Hills, 67
Whampoa Military Academy, 47
We P'ei-fu, General, 48
Wuhan, 58

Yalta, Summit Conference, 83
Yangtze River, Valley, 14, 16, 18, 26, 42, 50, 51, 58, 70, 85, 91
Yen, Y.C. James, 73
Yenan, Shensi Province, 60, 61
Yuan Shih-k'ai, General, 42, 43
Young Marshal, the (Chang Hsueh-liang), 51, 55, 61, 62, 63, 64, 65